D1328014

PROPHET OF INDIAN NATIONALISM

This work has been approved by the
University of Delhi
for the award of the degree of
Doctor of Philosophy

SRI AUROBINDO GHOSH (1872-1950)

PROPHET OF
INDIAN
NATIONALISM

A STUDY OF THE POLITICAL THOUGHT
OF SRI AUROBINDO GHOSH
1893—1910

By KARAN SINGH, M.A., Ph.D.

With a foreword by
Jawaharlal Nehru

London
GEORGE ALLEN & UNWIN LTD
RUSKIN HOUSE   MUSEUM STREET

PRINTED IN GREAT BRITAIN
in 11 *point Juliana type*
BY EAST MIDLAND PRINTING CO. LTD.
BURY ST. EDMUNDS

To Pandit Jawaharlal Nehru
in admiration and affection

FOREWORD

I HAVE read this little book with much interest and occasionally with some excitement. It brought to mind the days of my own boyhood and youth when Sri Aurobindo was writing his famous articles in the *Bande Mataram*. I was then at school in England and later at college in Cambridge, and was thus rather cut off from events in India which were seldom reported in England. Nevertheless, some news trickled through and the great anti-partition movement in Bengal filled us with enthusiasm. Among the famous figures of those days, Sri Aurobindo stood out and drew the admiration of the young. So reading about him in those days and, more particularly, his articles in the *Bande Mataram* have revived old memories.

It is extraordinary that a person who had spent fourteen of the most formative years of his life, from the age of 7 to 21, cut off from India and steeped in the European classics and the England of his day, should have become, in later years, the brilliant champion of Indian nationalism based on the philosophic and the spiritual background of Indian thought. His whole career in active politics was a very brief one, from 1905 to 1910 when he retired to Pondicherry and devoted himself to spiritual and yogic exercises. During these five years, he shone like a brilliant meteor and created a powerful impression on the youth of India. The great anti-partition movement in Bengal gained much of its philosophy from him and, undoubtedly, prepared the day for the great movements led by Mahatma Gandhi.

It is significant to note that great political mass movements in India have had a spiritual background behind them. In Sri Aurobindo s case, this was obvious, and his emotional appeals were based on intense nationalism and a concept of Mother India. Mahatma Gandhi's appeal to the people of India, to which they responded in an amazing degree, was essentially spiritual. Though it grew out of the background of India's philosophic heritage, it was addressed to the world.

Sri Aurobindo retired from politics at the early age of 38. Most of the people of my generation, who were immersed in political aspects of our struggle, did not understand why he did so. Later, when Gandhiji started his non-co-operation movements and convulsed India, we expected Sri Aurobindo to emerge from his retirement and join the great struggle. We were disappointed at his not doing so, though I have no doubt that all his good wishes were with it. During his retirement, he wrote, in his usual brilliant style, a number of books chiefly dealing with philosophic and religious subjects.

In commending this study of Sri Aurobindo's political thought, I would like to point out that the young man who has written it, is a scion of a princely house in India. At present, he is the elected Head or Governor of the State of Jammu and Kashmir. It is significant to note that he should have devoted himself to his studies and, more particularly, to this analysis of the political thought of Sri Aurobindo during a crucial period of our history, instead of occupying himself with the normal activities of Indian princes, that is, shikar, polo and high society.

JAWAHARLAL NEHRU
Prime Minister of India

Srinagar,
May, 1962

PREFACE

THIS work deals with the political thought of Sri Aurobindo Ghosh, covering the period from 1893—when he returned to India at the age of 21 after fourteen years in England—to 1910 when he abruptly left Calcutta for Chandernagore and later proceeded to Pondicherry. It thus covers eighteen years, which include a twelve-year preparatory phase during which he lived mainly in Baroda and a brief, though meteoric, career of active politics from 1905 to 1910.

The formation in 1885 of the Indian National Congress was an important landmark in the history of modern India. For several years after its birth it was dominated by the so-called 'Moderate' or 'Liberal' leaders, men of unexceptionable patriotism and ability such as Dadabhai Naoroji, Pherozeshah Mehta, Mahadev Govind Ranade, Rashbehari Ghosh and Gopal Krishna Gokhale. Despite their undoubted qualities, however, the 'Moderate' leaders were not able to galvanize and enthuse the vast masses of India because their approach to politics was extremely cautious and unexciting. The task of transforming the national movement from an intellectual pastime of a few into a mass movement was left to another group of leaders who came to be known as the 'Extremists' or 'Radicals'. This group contained some of the most extraordinary men that India has produced in modern times, including such giants as Bal Gangadhar Tilak, Lala Lajpat Rai, Bipin Chandra Pal and Sri Aurobindo Ghosh. Among these Sri Aurobindo was in many ways the most interesting personality. Famous later throughout the world as one of India's great Yogis and philosophers, and the creator of a profound and original system of thought, Aurobindo's role in the early phases of the national movement—though less well known —is important and deserves close study. From the literary and intellectual angle he was probably the most highly gifted of his distinguished contemporaries, and his writings throw a flood of light upon the political thought behind the radical movement in India at the turn of the century. Gifted with a highly sensitive and original mind, and an astonishing mastery over the English language, his political writings are almost unequalled for their deep spiritual fervour and flaming

9

nationalism. This work seeks to study his political thought during a crucial phase of modern Indian history.

Part I entitled 'The British Impact on India—the birth of Indian nationalism' is of an introductory nature. It seeks to outline the many-faceted impact which British rule had on India, and the renaissance to which this impact gave birth. The movements for social and religious reform that arose in Hindu society have been outlined, and I have sought to sketch the broad canvas against which Sri Aurobindo's contribution must be assessed.

Part II, 'Sri Aurobindo—the preparatory phase' is divided into three chapters. The first deals with his early life and the years of his youth spent in England, where nationalistic impulses first came to him when he was at Cambridge. The second chapter deals with his return to India in 1893 and his residence in Baroda for several years, during which his active political contacts began to develop. This period is important for his early political writings, specially his articles entitled 'New Lamps for Old' published in 1893-94 and his articles on Bankim Chandra Chatterjee published in 1894. It is in this period also that his active contacts with secret revolutionary societies were established. The third chapter deals with the favourable opportunity for the rapid growth of nationalism in India provided by the partition of Bengal in 1905 by Lord Curzon. This act created immense resentment in Bengal and paved the way for a rapid rise of radicalism there and in other parts of the country. It also impelled Sri Aurobindo to give up his veiled activities in Baroda and openly to enter the political fray.

Part III is entitled 'The philosophical basis of Sri Aurobindo's thought and his political goal'. In this Part I have dealt with Sri Aurobindo as an idealist, particularly with his theory of spiritual evolution which is a key concept in his thought. This leads directly to the heart of his political theory, which can be defined as 'spiritual nationalism'. Separate chapters have been devoted to his concept of nation, his concept of nationalism and his political goal of complete independence. These are all grounded upon his theory of the divinity of the motherland, which led him to look upon nationalism as a religion and upon the national movement as a religious *sadhana*.[1] This spiritual foundation of his political thought is of extreme importance in a proper assessment of his contribution, and the spiritual aspect, noticeable even in his early writings, grew more and more pronounced as the years went by.

Part IV deals with 'Sri Aurobindo as a radical leader—his technique of political action'. The first chapter deals with his general approach to political technique, and his rejection of the 'mendicant' policy of 'prayer, petition and protest' which he ascribed to the Moderates. The second chapter covers his attempt to bring about a revival of India's national spirit and pride in her great cultural heritage. Sri Aurobindo evidently felt that such a revival was essential if his programme of complete independence was to have any chance of success. The third chapter deals with his views on direct revolutionary action, including terrorism and armed revolt. His view that any means, including violence, were justified in delivering the motherland of her bondage has been clearly brought out. The fourth chapter deals with Sri Aurobindo's exposition of the theory of passive resistance and boycott. He was one of those rare individuals whose thought not only touched the heights of idealistic fervour, but also descended into the arena of practical politics and sought to prescribe a concrete scheme of action for attaining the political goal. Both the positive and negative sides of his theory have been stressed. Thus economic boycott has as a necessary corollary the development of Swadeshi; educational boycott the development of national education; judicial boycott the development of national arbitration courts; and executive boycott the development of national organization. And as the sanction behind these various types of boycott comes his theory of social boycott. As the background to the whole boycott movement I have brought in the broad political events of the crucial years from 1905 to 1910, including the Surat meeting of Congress where the split between the Moderates and the Extremists finally came to a head, and also the dramatic arrest, trial and acquittal of Sri Aurobindo in the celebrated Alipore Bomb Conspiracy case.

In this Part I have included a chapter of Sri Aurobindo's withdrawal from active politics in 1910. This has been very

[1] Discipline practiced for attainment of a spiritual goal.

much of a riddle, and many explanations have been given which include the allegation that he left due to frustration and fear of re-arrest. I have sought to show that in fact his withdrawal was the inevitable culmination of his inner spiritual development.

Finally, in *Part V*, I have attempted an assessment of Sri Aurobindo as a political thinker. A short bibliography of works referred to in the preparation of this book has been appended.

It remains for me to express my deep gratitude to the Prime Minister, Pandit Jawaharlal Nehru, for having, despite the immense pressure of work upon him, taken the trouble to go through the typescript of this work and write a foreword. The blessings of one of the greatest leaders of our times has been a source of great encouragement to me, and I have taken the liberty of dedicating this book to him.

K.S.

CONTENTS

PART I

THE BRITISH IMPACT ON INDIA

THE BIRTH OF MODERN INDIAN NATIONALISM

1

THE BRITISH IMPACT

In 1498 Vasco da Gama and his tiny fleet comprising three small vessels and a hundred and sixty men landed on Indian territory and cast anchor at Calicut, thus marking the beginning of a new epoch in the long and varied history of India. At the time the event passed almost unnoticed in the country, and indeed for many decades the Europeans were no more than unusually adventurous traders. The whole glory of the Mughal Empire in India lay yet in the future, and no one then could have dreamed that Vasco de Gama's landing was the forerunner of European domination over the entire Asian continent, based firmly upon their maritime supremacy. Yet this was in fact what transpired and when, just over two centuries later, Aurangzeb the last of the great Mughals died and the mighty structure of his Empire began to crumble, it was the Europeans who increasingly stepped into the void. The Portugese had by then been joined by the Dutch, the French and the British, all of whom eagerly sought to expand their trade with a great and wealthy India.

It is not possible here to attempt even the briefest summary of the tangled and tortuous disintegration of national unity in India during the eighteenth century, or of the rise, at first insiduous and finally rapid, of British power in the country. One by one, due in part to favourable fortune and in part to superior military and diplomatic skill, the British succeeded in ousting from the Indian scene the Portugese, the Dutch and the French. Finally, playing off local potentates against each other with consummate skill, they succeeded in establishing their sway over the entire sub-continent. By the time the nineteenth century dawned the British had become unquestioned masters of a vast Indian Empire. The larger part of the territory was directly administered by the East India Company, while about two-fifths was made up of the so-called Indian States whose rulers accepted the paramountcy of the British.

The British impact upon India was deep, many-sided and abiding. India had, during her long and often turbulent history, known many foreign invasions and incursions, though most of them were peripheral and left untouched the real centres of Indian polity. In fact, from one point of view, the whole panorama of Indian history can be viewed as an endless series of invasions followed by periods during which the invaders were assimilated into the vast cultural complex which they encountered. No doubt the process of assimilation was not always calm and peaceful, and often the invaders left a lasting impress upon the life of the sub-continent, but nevertheless they ended by becoming an integral part of the Indian scene and gradually lost touch with their foreign roots. This happened even in the case of the militant Islamic invasions that for centuries kept India in a state of constant turmoil. The Mughals, who represented the acme of Islamic power in India, were thoroughly Indianized. Despite their foreign origins and their cultural links with Iran and the Middle East they had become Indians and never looked upon themselves as outsiders.

With the British it was different. For the first time India fell under the rule of a people who were not only completely alien but whose seat of power was located many thousands of miles away and who showed no inclination to be assimilated into the Indian body-cultural. This peculiar circumstance, dictated as it was by the fact that the source of British power lay in her mastery over the seas, had certain peculiar effects upon the life and thought of India. The British impact on India had many facets, and, despite Britain's withdrawal in 1947, continues to exercise a very important influence even today. In the reaction to this impact may be sought the genesis of the great Indian Renaissance that began in the latter half of the nineteenth century and, at the dawn of the twentieth, led to the first truly modern nationalist upsurge in India. It is an interesting and ironic fact of history that the British impast was itself responsible for the creation of modern national consciousness in India which, in turn, led to the growth of the national movement that finally succeeded in ousting the British from India.

A pre-requisite for the growth of national consciousness in a vast sub-continent like India was a certain degree of unification, not only political but administrative, economic and intellectual. It was to a large extent the British impact that brought these

17

factors into being and thus paved the way for the rise of modern nationalism in India.

When the British entered the Indian political scene the country was in one of her periodic phases of turmoil. The grand Mughal Empire had disintegrated, and though several great Marhatta states held sway over large territories the country was by and large balkanized and administrative chaos was a common feature.[1] Through a series of political manoeuvres and military engagements the East India Company was able to establish its dominion over the whole country, and along with this political unification they imposed upon India an administrative system that increased in ability and efficiency until, by the end of the nineteenth century, it became widely accepted as one of the finest the world had ever known. There is no doubt that in many fields of administration, particularly revenue administration, the British merely took over with minor adaptations the system that had flourished under the Mughals. But the fact remained that they built up on an all-India basis a comprehensive executive-cum-judicial framework that was a powerful unifying factor.[2] In the sphere of law, particularly, the changes wrought by the British were nothing short of revolutionary. As Panikkar puts it in his masterly Survey of Indian History 'The establishment of the great principle of equality of all before law, in a country where under the Hindu doctrines a Brahmin could not be punished on the evidence of Sudras and even punishments varied according to caste, and where according to Muslim law an unbeliever's testimony could not be accepted against a Muslim, was itself a legal revolution of the first importance.[3]

The establishment of the great all-India services—the Indian Civil Service, the Indian Police Service, the Indian Audit & Accounts Service—as well as the Provincial services such as the Revenue and Judicial services, bound together the various units of this vast country in a manner never before attempted, and

---

[1] Cf K. M. Panikkar 'The Second half of the eighteenth century had witnessed over large areas of India a breakdown of civilization which has but few parallels in the history of the world'—A *Survey of Indian History* (Second Edition) p. 212.

[2] Cf Amaury de Reincourt 'Countless British officials and experts laboured to put together an impressive administrative machine with precise functions and codes, the first unifying cement in a land that had been split and divided time and again during its long history'. *The Soul of India* p. 206.

[3] A *Survey of Indian History* (Second Edition), pp. 204-5.

created the steel-frame within which the administrative unification of India became a reality. It must also be added that the
creation by the British of the Indian Army, though recruited
and officered by them mainly in their own interests, also proved
to be an integrating force. Recruited as it was from various parts
of the country, and organized on a non-political basis, the
Indian Army built up a glorious reputation on three continents
and provided free India with the basis of a national defence
force.

We may now glance at the economic impact of British rule.
Here the record is far less creditable than in the administrative
sphere, and it is clear that during the first century of British
rule there was wholesale economic exploitation of India which
resulted in her rapid impoverishment. We have become used to
the idea of India being an economically backward country, but
this was not always the case. Indeed for centuries India was
fabled throughout the world for her immense wealth, and it
was this that attracted to her the unwelcome attention of rapa-
cious invaders. At the time of the Mughal Empire India had a
flourishing export trade, and her products—silks, brocade,
cotton, salt, sugar and opium, to mention only a few—were
eagerly sought after in the markets of the world. Her handicrafts
were famous for their exquisite craftsmanship, and her inland
trade and commerce were also flourishing. In fact it would be
correct to say that in the period just preceding the Industrial
Revolution (which, ironically enough, received considerable
impetus by the influx into England of vast liquid funds as the
result of economic exploitation of India) India was among the
most highly advanced countries in the sphere of production,
trade and commerce. By the end of the first century of British
rule all this had changed. The entire Indian sub-continent had
been steadily impoverished by one of the most ruthless systems
of economic exploitation known to history.

It is not necessary here to deal in detail with this economic
factor.[1] Only a few salient features will be mentioned. Firstly, we
may take the sphere of agriculture, which then as now constituted the major economic activity of the Indian people. The out-

[1] Many Indian and foreign writers have analysed in great detail the
economic effects of British rule in India. See, for example, *Social Background
of Indian Nationalism* by A. K. Desai. The book, written incidentally from a
strictly Marxist viewpoint, gives a wealth of statistics to show the adverse
economic impact in India caused by British rule.

standing feature of the rural scene in India ever since earliest recorded history had been village self-sufficiency. The village was a complete, self-contained unit which catered to the social and economic needs of its inhabitants. It was characterized by a rigidly enforced caste structure based on a division of labour, and by the joint family system. Although the methods of agriculture were simple and primitive, the whole system did ensure an economic equilibrium at a low level. Socially and politically, the self-sufficient village provided an almost impregnable bulwark against change and upheaval, and through the centuries it maintained its structure intact despite the most drastic political vicissitudes. The British impact succeeded for the first time in destroying the age-old pattern of village self-sufficiency. What Britain required was the transformation of the Indian economy into a vast raw material producing system for British industry, and a huge market for mass-produced British goods. This was the very antithesis of self-sufficiency.

Soon after their advent the British introduced a radical change in the land tenure system. Whereas previously there existed a traditional right of the village community on village land, this was now superseded by two new systems—the Zemindari system whereby huge tracts were granted at fixed revenue rates to landlords (the celebrated Permanent Settlement of Cornwallis in 1793) and the Ryotwari system whereby the State dealt separately with each individual peasant. In both cases the old communal life of the village was disrupted, State courts supplanted village panchayats,[1] a money economy replaced the old system based largely on barter, and the whole pattern of Indian agriculture began to change. As against the old system of self-sufficiency, agriculture began to get commercialized and specialized. The peasants became victims of erratic fluctuations in the world market over which they had absolutely no control. A class of parasitic middle-men grew up who ruthlessly preyed on the peasant, and the money-lender became the symbol of this exploitation. The whole process, as can well be imagined, led to immense suffering among the peasantry who were steadily impoverished. Fragmentation of holdings, colossal rural indebtedness, fall in agricultural production, famines and pestilence all became regular features of the Indian rural scene.

In the sphere of industries the position was equally appalling.

[1] Village councils with administrative and judical functions.

The British made a concentrated effort to shatter indigenous industry, and as the result of intimidation and grossly unfair tariff policies they succeeded completely in this respect. The whole of India was flooded with cheap, machine-manufactured goods from British factories. Indian industry as well as village artisanship dwindled and vanished. In order to facilitate the export from India of raw material to Britain, as well as the distribution in India of British goods, a vast communications system was set up including both roads and railways.

It will thus be seen that the British economic impact on India was nothing short of disastrous. Nevertheless, even here it is obvious that the ultimate effect was to strengthen the unity of India. Despite the immense human suffering involved, it is clear that the system of atomized village communities was outmoded and had to go if India was to become a modern, unified State. By breaking down this self-sufficiency and for the first time creating what might be called a national economy, the British made an important contribution towards laying the foundations for the growth of true national consciousness in India. The opening up of the interior and the linking up of various parts of the country by a network of railways also had a similar effect. Thus out of evil good arose, and the very destruction and exploitation of the Indian economy by the British helped ultimately in bringing about the birth of modern Indian nationalism.

We have seen how the political, administrative and economic impact of British rule all conduced towards the creation of Indian unity and subsequently the birth of a truly modern national consciousness. Another equally important, and perhaps even more pervasive, aspect was the intellectual impact. The main vehicle through which this developed was the introduction of the English language into Indian education.

It has been rightly remarked that 'no single act of British policy has had a more lasting influence on the evolution of modern Indian thought than the decision in 1835 to use Governmental funds to support education in the English language and to adopt the curriculum prevalent in English schools.'[1] This had a profound effect upon the future development of Indian politics and in fact on almost all facets of Indian life, as it greatly accelerated the diffusion among the Indian intelligentsia of Western ideas and modes of thought. Falling as

[1] S. N. Hay in *Sources of Indian tradition* (Columbia) pp. 587-88.

it did upon the fertile and profound Indian mind, it acted as a catalytic agent that caused an immense upsurge of creative thought and activity.

In her periods of greatest glory India was always receptive to fresh ideas and impulses, always willing to imbide what was best in foreign cultures. Thus the famous words of the Rigveda:

'Let noble thoughts come to us from every side'.[1] Such creative periods, however, were often followed by a reaction, a narrowing down of the great universal vision, an obscurantist and puerile phase. Thus at one time we find Indian monks and missionaries, traders and princes, going on missions of peace across the oceans carrying with them to all the lands of Asia the great culture and civilization of India; while at another we find the spirit so narrowed that a trip abroad was believed to make the traveller impure and necessitated elaborate purifactory rites on his return before he could be accepted back into society! At the time of the British impact India was in one of the latter phases. The true glory of Hinduism—with its sublime philosophical doctrines—was sicklied over with narrow caste and social restrictions, absurd superstitions and taboos. What was needed was a gust of fresh air from outside which would clear away the cobwebs and reveal the handsome structure beneath. The advent of English education fulfilled this important task. Although doubtless geared mainly towards producing a class of 'babus' who would act as intermediaries between the British and their Indian subjects, it at the same time brought to the best Indian minds new ideas and concepts, a new intellectual awakening that sparked off the great Indian revival.[2]

It is also important to stress here that English education by no means caused Indians to forego their ancient cultural heritage. Although, as we shall see later, some people did react in a nihilistic sort of fashion, by and large it led to a better appreciation by Indians of their past glories and attainments. The great Orientalists, such as Sir William Jones who, along with Cole-

---

[1] *Rig Veda* 1-89-1.

[2] The credit for the introduction of English, as well as the great legal code that he gave to India, goes to Thomas Babington Macaulay. His sneering references to the value of Indian classical literature—born of his almost total ignorance in this realm—should not obscure the fact that he was one of the great builders of modern India. His celebrated Minute on Education (1835) and the bitter controversy with the Orientalists led by Sir William Jones, are a fascinating chapter in modern Indian history.

brooke, established the Bengal Asiatic Society in 1783 and whose translation of *Kalidasa's* classic *Shakuntala* was a landmark in the rise of European interest in Indian culture, have earned from all Indians a lasting debt of gratitude for their pioneering work in the field of re-discovering India's great intellectual heritage. As one historian aptly puts it:

'Although the Orientalists were defeated on the question of educational policy, their high evaluation of India's classical heritage helped eventually to foster in English-educated Indians a pride in their own past which was of cardinal importance in the nineteenth century renaissance of Hinduism and the rise of Hindu nationalism.'[1]

British archaeologists and philologists helped greatly in the immense task of bringing to light India's past. The work of such men as James Princep, who in 1834 discovered the clue to the Ashokan inscriptions; Alexander Cunningham and Fergusson who did pioneering work in the study of Indian architecture and archaeology; Dr. Hultz who, as epigraphist to the Government of India, rendered valuable service in the deciphering of ancient Indian scripts; and later men like Monier Williams and the great German savant Max Müller—all combined to bring to light the long and distinguished history of India and her great achievements in numerous realms of human activity.[2] This, along with a knowledge of the English language, caused an immense intellectual ferment in India, and led to a rebirth among Indian intellectuals of pride in their national heritage. As we shall see constantly throughout this work, this was an extremely important element in the growth of Indian nationalism that began at the end of the nineteenth century and swept

[1] *Sources of Indian Tradition*, p. 590.

[2] Cf Panikkar in *Commonsense about India* pp. 24-25. After mentioning the great Indologists he goes on to add that French and Dutch scholars working in Indo-China and Indonesia, as also great Chinese scholars like Pelliot and Sylvian Levy, revealed to the world conclusive evidence of the penetration of Indian culture into the Far East. He concludes with the remark that 'By the first decade of the twentieth century, the achievement of the Hindu people had become—let it be remembered, as a result primarily of the work of European scholars—a source of pride to the Hindus. A new national image came into being, and the Hindus began to see themselves as a people who had not only contributed to the thought of the world, but had in their time been the carriers of civilization and the builders of empire in far off lands.'

to a triumphant conclusion before the middle of the twentieth.

Finally, the introduction of English education created a new educated elite cutting across caste and provincial barriers. This new English-educated class, imbued with Western ideas of democracy and freedom, provided one of the most important unifying elements in the Indian body politic and, to an amazing extent, supplied the leadership in the nationalist movement that swept the country. Thus, as one Western commentator puts it:

'—the English education which provided so many willing collaborators for the British in India eventually proved the undoing of their empire. For one thing, the members of the new middle class—whether from the South or the North, from Bengal or from Maharashtra—could all communicate with each other through the medium of a common language. Equally important, their reading of the English classics instilled in them the Western ideals of justice, freedom and love of country.'[1]

It should also be noted that, as Panikkar remarks, English was 'in fact the language of Hindu reformation and without it, though the Hindu religion would no doubt have been reformed and society reorganized, the movement would have been regional and the unity of India would have been further broken up.'[2] It is significant that some of the greatest figures in the Hindu reformation, such as Vivekananda, Sri Aurobindo, Gandhiji and Radhakrishnan, wrote largely—if not exclusively—in English.

Thus, by and large, the British impact in India was highly conducive to the growth of Indian unity and the subsequent birth of modern Indian nationalism. There is no doubt that the loss by any country of its freedom is always a disaster, nor can one deny the fact of cruel economic exploitation by the conquerors. But the political, administrative, economic and intellectual unification of India that flowed from the British impact were an essential pre-requisite to the rise of Indian nationalism. The next chapter will try and study the various Indian reactions to this impact.

[1] *Sources of Indian Tradition* p. 661.

[2] *Commonsense about India* by K. M. Panikkar, p. 24.

THE INDIAN RENAISSANCE

—MOVEMENTS FOR SOCIAL AND RELIGIOUS REFORM

THE reaction to a many-sided impact is also bound to be rich and varied, particularly when the receiving civilization is one of the most ancient and profound in the history of Mankind. The British impact on India led ultimately to an amazing recovery and resurgence among the conquered. It is extremely difficult in a short span even to begin to do justice to this historical phenomenon, and this chapter is confined to outlining a few broad features to indicate the nature of the Indian revival which led to the development of modern Indian nationalism in which Sri Aurobindo was destined to play such a dramatic role.

When we talk of the Indian revival, we refer mainly to the revival among the Hindus. This does not in any way deprecate the importance of the other communities, particularly the Muslims, who inhabited this vast sub-continent. It merely reflects the obvious fact that the vast majority of Indians, then as now, were Hindus. It is also true that throughout her long history, at least the era subsequent to the great Aryan influx, it is Hinduism that set the tone of national culture in India, that acted as the great creative force behind most of her varied achievements, that provided the ethos, the cultural milieu, the great backdrop, as it were, against which the drama of her history was played out. It is true that the great heresies of Buddhism and Jainism sought at times to break away from the Hindu fold, but they never succeeded in completely repudiating their creatrix. It is also true that the stern creed of Islam swept across most of North India and for centuries dominated the political life thereof, but the vast masses of India continued largely to accept their traditional religion, and even Islam was to some extent modified due to its impact with Hinduism.

Furthermore, Hinduism for the people of India had, through

the centuries, been not merely a formal religion but a whole way of life, a zeitgeist influencing and motivating every aspect of individual and cultural life. Political activity was always considered only a single and hence strictly limited facet of corporate life in India, and it would have been unrealistic to expect a political awakening without a deep stirring with the vast body of Hinduism itself. Sri Aurobindo has at one place written that 'All great movements of life in India have begun with a new spiritual thought and usually a new religious activity.'[1] This maxim certainly held true for the great Indian revival in the nineteenth century. As we shall see, it was with Hindu reform movements that the renaissance began, subsequently pushing inexorably forward towards political emancipation.

The British conquest at one stroke changed the relationship between the two great communities of India, the Hindus and the Muslims. Prior to their advent the Muslims had for many centuries been the ruling class in large parts of India, though towards the end of the Mughal Empire the Marhattas and the Rajputs had begun to re-assert their traditional independence. With the coming of the British, however, both Hindus and Muslims were equalized under foreign rule, and though they lost their freedom they were inter se placed on the same level. This acted distinctly in favour of the Hindu, who, with his greater familiarity with and ability in trade and commerce, soon began to work in profitable concert with the 'nation of shop-keepers'. The Muslims, being the holders of power prior to the British advent, were naturally looked upon with suspicion by the new rulers, and the remark of Lord Ellenborough in an official communication to London that the Muslims were fundamentally hostile and that Britain's true policy was to reconcile the Hindus was typical of the early British attitude. Furthermore, with their greater intellectual resilience, the Hindus soon began to forge ahead, while the Muslims remained for a long time aggrieved, disheartened and depressed.

In 1857 came the great upheaval, known variously as the

[1] *The Renaissance in India* p. 44. Cf. the statement of a modern Western historian 'Awakening can take place only on the plane on which consciousness still dwells. This explains that the most powerful agent of metamorphosis in depth could only be the profound philosophic bent and religious feeling which is so much part of India that its disappearance would destroy the very soul of that great country'—A. de Reincourt in *The Soul of India* p. 227.

Indian Mutiny and the First Indian War of Independence.[1] For
a short while the hold of the British was shaken and it seemed
as if they would be expelled. But though the various uprisings
—in which, incidentally, Hindus and Muslims joined hands
against the foreign invader—were prompted by the same sentiments and produced some leaders of note, there was no central
co-ordination, and after an initial period of shock the British
with their superior central direction and policy were able to
crush the movement. The event, however, though unsuccessful
was pregnant with significance for the future history of India.
As Panikkar remarks, 'In the first place it was the last effort of
the old order to regain national independence and honour, and
though stained by cruelty, it was a heroic effort of a dispossessed
people to re-assert their national dignity. In the second place, it
is the Great Divide in modern Indian history, as the policy,
practice and ideals of the Government that followed differed
fundamentally from the Government of the company which it
displaced. The Crown took over the Government of India in
1858, and the East India Company vanished from the stage of
history.'[2]

After the Mutiny, thinking Indians realized that the British
could not so easily be shaken off, and that other methods would
be required based on a regeneration of the Indian spirit itself. In
the meantime there were stirrings within the great body of Hin-
ism as the Leviathan began to awake from its torpor. It is to this
aspect that we will now turn.

Bengal was the first Province in India to feel the brunt of the
British conquest, and this fact, allied with the extraordinary
emotional and intellectual gifts of the Bengalis, naturally led to
Bengal becoming the centre of the cultural revival. And it was in
Bengal that there arose the first in a long series of great leaders
of thought and action, a man who has often been described as
the father of modern India, Raja Rammohun Roy (1772-1833).
The Raja was a man of unusual intellectual ability, a profound
scholar of Sanskrit and Persian as well as a deep admirer of
British culture. He was one of those who felt that India had

---

[1] The former term has been popularized by the British, but many Indian
historians prefer the latter. The centenary in 1957 of the great revolt was
the occasion for considerable research into and re-interpretation of this important event in modern Indian history.

[2] *Survey of Indian History* (2nd Edition) p. 203.

everything to gain from contact with the West, and he strove to imbide the best that the West had to offer. He took a leading part in founding English-medium schools in Bengal—several at his own expense—through which the youth of Bengal could acquire the most modern Indian education. In 1823 the Government decided to support a new college for Sanskrit studies, and his famous letter[1] of protest to the Governor-General Lord Amherst showed how deeply he supported the introduction into India of Western learning. The communication, couched in superb English, later provided powerful ammunition to the Anglicists led by Macaulay in their struggle against the Orientalists.

The life and career of Raja Rammohun Roy was extremely varied and interesting,[2] but the main act for which he is remembered was his founding in 1828 the Brahmo Sabhā, which eighteen years later was developed by Maharshi Debendranath Tagore into the Brahmo Samāj. This organization marked the first deliberate attempt in modern India to reform Hinduism and, shearing off its unessential and often undesirable growths, to restore it to its pristine glory. In the Trust Deed of the Brahmo Sabha the Raja dedicated it 'for the worship and adoration of the eternal unsearchable and immutable Being who is the Author and Preserver of the Universe.' His reform of Hinduism was based on his own highly controversial interpretation of the Vedas and the Upanishadas, and, like Swami Dayananda after him, he strongly attacked idolatry. The Raja and many of his followers, notably Keshub Chander Sen, were deeply influenced by Christianity.

An important point to note is that the early reform movements, including the Brahmo Samāj and the various societies into which it broke up after the death of the founder, laid their

[1] *English Works* pp. 471-74.

[2] Well summed up by de Reincourt as follows: 'Rammohun Roy's fantastic knowledge and amazing life symbolized this very synthesis for which he laboured all his life: steeped in both Hindu and Muslim cultures, fluent in Arabic, Persian, Sanskrit, English, Hebrew, Greek and Latin, expelled for a time by caste and family, having lived for years thereafter in Benaras and Tibet, he finally returned home in 1796 and set about his life's work. Campaigning tirelessly against the monstrous distortions which centuries of sloth, corruption and inertia had inflicted on Hinduism (such as *sati*, the self-immolation of widows, which he finally persuaded the British authorities to ban), he tackled every social, political and cultural problem of his time.' (*Soul of India*, p. 230).

main stress on social reform, on purging Hindu society of the absurd aberrations that had entered it during the long centuries of Muslim rule and even before. Their emphasis on political matters was slight. In fact the Raja once remarked 'When we have to depend by the very conditions of our existence on all things and all beings in nature, is not this fiery love of national independence a chimera . . . India requires many more years of British domination. . . .' In this the early social reformers might well be considered the intellectual progenitors of the later 'Liberals' in the Congress, who placed social and economic reform above political emancipation.

We have mentioned Debendranath Tagore as an associate of Raja Rammohun Roy. After the Raja's death Tagore took up the leadership of the reform movement. A man of deep learning and spiritual poise, the Maharshi (Saint, as he came to be called) wielded great intellectual authority in the Samāj. In 1862, however, there appeared on the scene the third great theistic reformer of Bengal, a brilliant young man named Keshub Chander Sen. Sen was at this period of his life deeply influenced by Christianity, and he gathered around him a group of younger men who were zealous not only in propagating the reform of Hinduism but also in social service such as famine relief. Gradually, however, a rift grew between the old conservative group of the Samāj and the younger reformers led by Sen.[1] Finally the split occurred, the old party still led by Debendranath Tagore shrunk to the Ādi Brahmo Samāj, while Keshub Chander Sen founded in 1868 the Brahmo Samāj of India.

It is not necessary here to enter into a detailed survey of the activities of these Societies. In 1871 Sen died at the early age of forty-six, and in 1878 the Sādharan Brahmo Samāj was founded by some of his followers. Earlier, under Sen's influence, the Prārthana Samāj had been formed in Bombay in 1867 by two great figures of Western India, Ranade and Bhandarkar. The influence of these humane and enlightened societies was considerable, particularly in Bengal and Maharashtra. They helped to bring about an intellectual awakening among the intelligentsia in both these provinces, and threw up men of great ability and erudition who played distinguished roles in the early phase of the national movement. Their limitation was that being

---

[1] See article on the Brahmo Samāj by Dr Kalidas Nag in *The Cultural Heritage of India* (The Ramakrishna Mission Institute of Culture), Vol. IV.

opposed to traditional Hinduism they could not create any mass enthusiasm.

We must now turn to another remarkable nineteenth century figure in India, a man described by Sri Aurobindo as 'one of its great and formative spirits', Swami Dayananda Saraswati. Unlike the Brahmo Samāj with its leanings towards Christianity, the Ārya Samāj founded by Dayananda in 1875 was a true Hindu Protestant Reformation. Dayananda passionately advocated a return to the pristine purity of Vedic Hinduism, and denounced with intolerant indignation all post-Vedic Hindu scriptures such as the *Puranas*, the *Brahmanas* and even the *Upanishadas*. He thus attacked *Vedantism*, *Tantricism* and popular Pauranic Hinduism with equal vehemence, and his turbulent ministry caused a sharp upheaval in Hindu society. At the same time he condemned caste distinctions, advocated full equality for women, launched a violent campaign against untouchability and started a widespread and remarkably successful educational campaign mainly in the Punjab and Uttar Pradesh. The influence of Swami Dayananda, a remarkable human dynamo endowed with extraordinary power and energy, was immense. His Ārya Samāj succeeded in shaking the whole structure of Hinduism in the Punjab and infusing into it new blood and vigour in a manner which the Brahmo-Samājists never achieved.[1]

The political overtones of the Ārya Samāj movement were also much more marked than those of the Brahmo Samāj. In fact de Reincourt goes as far as to say that 'there is little doubt today that the great revolt in Bengal in 1905 was largely the indirect result of the Ārya Samāj's religious nationalism, and that Dayananda's organization was the first real concrete nucleus of political nationalism.'[2] The Ārya Samāj showed that Hinduism, long hibernating in a self-enclosed world of its own, was beginning rapidly to awake and face the realities of the nineteenth century. It also revealed that there was fire within the great body of Hinduism which, if struck by a competent hand, could be coaxed into a blaze of life and energy. The concept of the gentle and often servile Hindu began to disappear.

Nevertheless, like the Brahmo Samāj, the appeal of the Ārya Samāj was also mainly intellectual and, as it also attacked the

[1] In fact the Ārya Samāj is to this day a potent force, both cultural and political, specially in the Punjab.

[2] *The Soul of India*, p. 236.

main body of traditional Hinduism, its appeal was limited to certain sections and areas of Hindu Society. A mention may be made here of another religious movement which, though born abroad, was based largely on Hindu doctrines and was introduced into India towards the end of the nineteenth century. The Theosophical Society, founded by Madame Blavatsky and Colonel Olcott in New York in 1875, drew profusely from the occult and cabalistic elements in Tibetan Buddhism, as well as Hindu modes of thought. For a while Theosophy gained quite a vogue both in the West and in India. It did valuable service by its extensive translations into English of Hindu scriptures, and thus contributed towards reviving in English-educated Hindus faith in their ancient sacred literature. With Mrs Annie Besant, Theosophy became directly linked with the political Home Rule movement, and there is no doubt that this curious eclectic creed had a beneficial and revivifying effect upon Hindu society at a crucial period of its history, and helped in its regeneration.

A truly organic and fundamental revival of Hinduism, however, had necessarily to come from within the general body of Hindu tradition. This was destined to be the life work of two of the most remarkable figures in the religious history of the world—Sri Ramakrishma and Swami Vivekananda. The life and teachings of these two spiritual giants constitute a fascinating and inspiring chapter in the history of modern Indian thought.[1] Here we must confine ourselves to pointing out the tremendous impact that the Saint of Dakshineshwar and his great disciple had on the mind of contemporary India, an impact that even half a century after the latter's death has lost none of its depth and power.

Sri Ramakrishna (1836-1886) was born in a poor Brahmin family living at the humble village of Kamarpukur in the Hoogly District of West Bengal. At an early age he began showing unusual signs of religious ecstasy, and when he was only 19 he came to Calcutta to live with his brother who had been appointed priest of a newly erected temple near the city. This extensive temple, founded by one Rani Rasmani, was at Dakshineshwar on the banks of the Ganga and had shrines dedicated to Shiva and Krishna. But the main temple was dedicated to the great Goddess Kāli, and it was as a devotee of the

---

[1] The literature on them is profuse. Among others, Romain Rolland wrote biographies both of Sri Ramakrishna and Swami Vivekananda.

Goddess that Sri Ramakrishna began his astounding career of spiritual disciplines and attainments.

The concept of Kāli is a profound one, and has deeply influenced generations of Hindus down through the long vistas of Indian history. She symbolizes the great cosmic Becoming, in contradistinction to—though inevitably and eternally united with—the great cosmic Being symbolized by Shiva. She thus combines within Herself two aspects: to her enemies, to those who throw their lot against the spiritual path and cut themselves off from the true source of light and power, She presents a fierce and terrifying visage; while to her devotees, to those who seek union with the true spiritual source of their being, She has all the love and tenderness of a divine and gracious mother. That the same symbol can combine within itself two so diametrically opposed concepts is often a source of bewilderment to observers who are unacquainted with the depth and profundity of Hindu symbology. It is of interest to remark that Kāli, known also by the terms Bhawāni, Bhavatārini, Durgā etc., has been the favourite deity of most of the Hindu leaders who have sought to free India from the bonds of enslavement, if necessary by force. Thus we find the great Marhatta warrior Shivaji, the Rajput heroes of Rajputana, the terrorists and extremists of Bengal at the turn of the century including Sri Aurobindo,[1] all seeking to derive strength and courage from the mighty Goddess.

Sri Ramakrishna, during his stay at Dakshineshwar, experienced profound spiritual developments. Visions, trances, ecstasies crowded in upon him, and most of his time was spent in spiritual rhapsodies. His intense craving to see God face to face was finally fulfilled, and he then proceeded, under various spiritual guides, to experience the whole gamut of mystical relationship described in the Hindu scriptures, ranging from the most intense emotional transports to the highest sublime quietude of the Nirvikalpa Samādhi—absorption in the supreme, unmanifested Bramhan which is the final goal of Vedānta. Then he proceeded to adopt the spiritual practices of Islam and Christianity, and in both cases this culminated in rewarding spiritual experiences.

[1] In fact, as we shall see later in this work, Sri Aurobindo's plan for a secret society to train revolutionary sanyasis was dedicaed to Bhawāni, and the concept of the Goddess as the source of power (Shakti) is elaborated in his celebrated pamphlet on 'Bhawāni Mandir'.

The cumulative effect of all these extraordinary phenomena was immense. On the one hand they brought him the first-hand and overpowering realization that all spiritual paths within and without Hinduism, if correctly followed, lead to the same goal, a doctrine enunciated in the Vedas millennia earlier.[1] On the other they spread his fame far and wide, and this illiterate young Bengali priest from an obscure Hoogly village began to attract to himself the footsteps of an incredibly varied assortment of people. The rich and the poor, the educated and the illiterate, the villager and the Calcutta city dweller, all began to be drawn to Dakshineshwar. In Hinduism, the supreme veneration has always been reserved for saints who have *realized* the spiritual goal. Learning and erudition have commanded respect, but never by themselves have they been sufficient to elicit veneration. It is the spiritually realized saint—be he prince or pauper, learned pandit or illiterate weaver, royal princess or naked yogin—who in Hinduism has received the supreme adoration. And this explains why Ramakrishna attracted to his abode an unending stream of humanity.

Among the many who came to him were the greatest literary and cultural figures of contemporary Bengal—men like Michael Madhusudan Dutt, Ishwar Chandra Vidyasagar, Debendranath Tagore and the brilliant Keshub Chander Sen who came into intimate association with the saint. And to all who came Ramakrishna gave the same message—waste not your time in partisan squabbles over the superiority of this or that creed, or this or that religion, but seek God with a pure and dedicated heart. He showed by his practical example that Hinduism was by no means an archaic and dying religion, as some of the newly educated intelligentsia had begun to believe, but an inexhaustible fount of true spirituality. Acting as a mighty spiritual beacon Sri Ramakrishna, though continuing to live quietly at Dakshineshwar, generated a powerful current of fresh life into Hindu society. He was not concerned with caste or creed, with empty ceremonies or shallow rituals. He was the apostle of divine realization, one of those rare souls who appear from time to time and create a spiritual revolution.[2]

---

[1] Cf. 'Truth is One, the wise call it by many names'. (*Rig. Veda* 1. 164. 46.)

[2] It is interesting and fascinating to see how, throughout her long and complex history, India has constantly produced such men and women who kept the torch of spirituality burning even during her darkest periods. In

C

Apart from his influence on his contemporaries, Sri Rama-krishna also attracted to his feet a group of brilliant young disciples, most of them products of the new English schools and colleges that had been established in Bengal. These young men, many of whom had lost faith in their traditional culture and were wallowing in a sea of cynicism and spiritual despair, found in the master a haven, a source of immense power and inspira-tion that banished their spiritual bankruptcy and transformed their very personalities. Outstanding among these disciples was one Narendranath Dutta, later famous the world over as the great Swami Vivekananda.

Just before his passing away, Sri Ramakrishna specifically designated Swami Vivekananda as his spiritual heir, and after the Master's death in 1886 he took upon himself the task of knitting the disciples into a homogeneous and dedicated body. Vivekananda was a man of remarkable qualities, gifted alike with a powerful physique and an outstanding intellect. Though apparently poles apart from the Master in every respect—physi-cally, temperamentally, educationally, intellectually—Vivekan-anda fell under the influence of Sri Ramakrishna and thus created one of the most celebrated teacher-disciple relationships since Socrates and Plato. And as in the case of the great Greeks, it was the student who spread the teachings of his master far and wide until they traversed almost the entire civilized world.

Vivekananda soon got an ideal opportunity to make use of his exceptional talents. After Sri Ramakrishna's passing he had wandered as a *Sanyasi*[1] over the entire length of India seeking the path which he should tread, the method by which he could propagate the ideals of his beloved master. In 1892 he heard of the Parliament of Religions that was to be held in Chicago in 1893 in connection with the World Fair. With some difficulty he managed to get a passage to America and, after facing numerous rebuffs and disappointments, finally reached Chicago and succeeded in getting himself enrolled as a delegate to the Parliament of Religions.

His advent at the gathering had all the elements of high

fact this is one of the secrets of the continuance of her culture through the long vista of history. Whereas ancient Egypt, ancient Greece, ancient Rome are dead, India maintains a living and vital link with the dawn of her history.

[1] An ochre-robed ascetic who has renounced worldly life.

34

drama. An unknown and obscure Indian, he succeeded by the very force of his personality in dominating the whole concourse, which today is remembered mainly because of him. His famous address on the first day of the Parliament, in which he addressed the audience as 'Sisters and brothers of America' created a sensation in the great assembly, and his subsequent addresses confirmed him as an outstanding religious preacher. As the *New York Herald* put it, he was 'undoubtedly the greatest figure in the Parliament of Religions', adding somewhat ruefully that 'After hearing him, we feel how foolish it is to send missionaries to this learned nation.'

Vivekananda brought to the West the true message of Hinduism, the real spiritual essence and not the mumbo jumbo that the West had so often mistaken for Hinduism. The sublime doctrines of Vedanta found in his words chaste and eloquent expression. After a triumphant tour in the United States as well as in England he returned to India in 1897, where a hero's welcome awaited him. Reports of his great success in the West had poured into India during his absence, creating in his countrymen a new sense of pride in their great spiritual heritage. True, the West might be more advanced in the scientific and technological fields, but Vivekananda's amazing *tour de force* had shown that in the field of spiritual truths India was the eternal guru.

On his return to India the Swami undertook again a tour from Kanya Kumari to Kashmir, this time not as an itinerant monk but as a triumphant spiritual teacher. His lectures delivered during this tour are remarkable for their passionate eloquence, deeply charged with love for India and its oppressed and teeming millions. An acute awareness of the social and economic degradation of the Indian masses, despite their sublime cultural heritage, was a marked feature of Vivekananda's speeches. In lecture after lecture he thundered against this degradation, against the monstrous excesses practised in the name of Hinduism, against the cruel caste barriers that shamed the fair name of Mother India, against the oppression of women. But his words were never merely destructive. While unflinching in his contempt for the 'kitchen religion' with its fantastic taboos that passed under the name of Hinduism, he simultaneously held up before his listeners the glorious image of India's true spiritual greatness. As a modern commentator puts it:

'With the same breath the Swami made them discover the infinite potentialities that still lay hidden in the depth of their hearts beneath the superficial film of filth and degradation, and they were made to visualize the bright and glorious days of a thoroughly rejuvenated future India.'[1]

In fact what Vivekananda achieved was nothing short of a complete restatement and re-interpretation of Hinduism in the light of modern conditions and requirements. Through his writings and speeches the new English-educated intelligentsia that held the key to the future of India rediscovered the tremendous strength of their ancient religion, the spiritual treasures that lay all around them. Where previously there had been cold scepticism there now arose fresh hope and inspiration. Swami Vivekananda passed away in 1902 at the young age of thirty-nine, but before he did so he had wrought a virtual revolution. He founded in 1897 the Ramakrishna Mission with its headquarters at Belur near Calcutta, and from then onwards right up to this day this dedicated society has spread throughout India and the world, carrying with it the enlightened and inspiring gospel of Sri Ramakrishna and his great disciple.

The political implications of Vivekananda's ministry are not far to seek. Though not openly allied with any political group, the whole tenor of his teaching was directed towards bringing about a profound resurgence in Hindu society. For the first time the masses were touched,[2] and for the first time a reform movement grew from out of the very heart of traditional Hinduism. This could not fail to have deep political repercussions, and we find that many of the great nationalist leaders such as Tilak and Aurobindo were profoundly influenced by Vivekananda. If Rammohun Roy can be described as the intellectual progenitor of the Liberals, Vivekananda is the spiritual progenitor of the Radicals. Several concepts later developed by Radical leaders are to be found in Vivekananda's writings: the fundamental importance of religion in India's national life ('In India, religious

[1] Swami Nirvedananda in his masterly article on 'Sri Ramakrishna and Spiritual Renaissance', *The Cultural Heritage of India* (Ramakrishna Mission Institute of Culture) Vol. IV.

[2] Cf. '(Vivekananda) gave his countrymen an added sense of dignity and pride in their own culture. His zeal to serve the down-trodden masses opened a new dimension of activity to Indian nationalist leaders, whose Western outlook had heretofore isolated them from the vast majority of their countrymen'. *Sources of Indian Tradition* (Columbia) p. 647.

life forms the centre, the key-note of the whole music of national life'); the primacy of spiritual over social reform ('Meddle not with so-called social reform, for there cannot be any reform without spiritual reform first'), the doctrine that India has a predestined goal to give spiritual light to the world and must for this reason recover her great heritage;[1] in short the utmost importance of a complete recovery of cultural self-consciousness of the Hindu community. de Reincourt beautifully sums up the great influence of Vivekananda when he writes 'The greatest leaders of the early twentieth century, whatever their walk of life—Rabindranath Tagore, the prince of poets; Aurobindo Ghose, the greatest mystic-philosopher; Mahatma Gandhi, who eventually shook the Anglo-Indian Empire to destruction—all acknowledged their over-riding debt to both the Swan and the Eagle, to Ramakrishna who stirred the heart of India, and to Vivekananda who awakened its soul.'[2]

We thus see that the nineteenth century witnessed a profound renaissance in India, brought about mainly as the result of the British impact. The great social reform leaders and movements—Rammohun Roy and Debendranath Tagore of the Brahmo Samāj, Keshub Chander Sen of the Brahmo Samāj of India, Bhandarkar and Ranade of the Prārthana Samāj, Dayananda of the Ārya Samāj, Blavatsky and Annie Besant of the Theosophical Society, and Sri Ramakrishna and Swami Vivekananda all combined to bring about an intellectual, social, cultural and spiritual ferment which shook Hindu society to its depths, and inevitably gave birth to a national movement of political re-generation.

In 1893, the year Vivekananda addressed the Parliament of Religions in Chicago, Sri Aurobindo returned to India after spending fourteen years in England. Having sketched the broad canvas against which he started his adult life in India, we will in subsequent chapters seek to trace the growth of his political ideas arising from his brief, though dramatic and profoundly significant, career in active Nationalist politics.

[1] Cf. 'Vivekananda's reinterpretation of Hinduism to bring it into harmony with modern requirements developed the idea that though India should learn practical knowledge from the West, she must teach the materialistic West her ancient and sublime religious wisdom.' *Sources of Indian Tradition* (Columbia) p. 658.

[2] *The Soul of India*, p. 250.

PART II

SRI AUROBINDO

THE PREPARATORY PHASE

3

EARLY LIFE AND YOUTH IN ENGLAND

SRI AUROBINDO was born in Calcutta on August 15, 1872, the
third son of Dr Krishnadhan Ghose and Shrimati Swaranlata
Devi.[1] His father was a Civil Surgeon and had received his
advanced medical training in England. He was evidently a man
of great ability and strong personality, and after his return from
England he refused the demand of the orthodox sections of his
village—Konnagar in the Hoogly district of West Bengal—that
he should perform *prayashchitta* or purification for having
travelled beyond the seas. This absurd custom, so alien to the
true spirit of Hinduism which centuries ago had sent cultural
ambassadors across the oceans and lands of South East Asia, was
typical of the narrow sectarianism that had developed in India
as the result of many centuries of alien rule. Dr Ghose preferred
to leave his village for good rather than submit to the ritual.

It is an important fact, throwing much light on Sri Aurobindo's educational career, that his father returned from England deeply impressed by the English way of life. To quite Sri
Aurobindo's own words:

'He returned entirely anglicized in habits, ideas and ideals,—
so strongly that Aurobindo as a child spoke English and
Hindustani only and learned his mother-tongue only after his
return from England. He was determined that his children
should receive an entirely European upbringing. While in India
they were sent for the beginning of their education to an Irish
Nun's school in Darjeeling and in 1879 he took his three sons

---

[1] In this context, only a brief account of his early life and youth will be
given. For further details his biographers may be consulted, specially *Sri
Aurobindo* by K. R. Srinivasa Iyengar, *Life of Sri Aurobindo* and *Sri
Aurobindo in England* by A. B. Purani, *Mahayogi* by R. R. Diwakar and *Sri
Aurobindo and his Ashram* published from Pondicherry. The chapter in
Sri Aurobindo on himself and on the Mother (Pondicherry) entitled 'Early
life in England' is also of much value, coming as it does from the pen of Sri
Aurobindo himself.

to England and placed them with an English Clergyman and his wife with strict instructions that they should not be allowed to make the acquaintance of any Indian or undergo any Indian influence. These instructions were carried out to the letter and Aurobindo grew up in entire ignorance of India, her people, her religion and her culture.'[1]

Thus at the age of seven Sri Aurobindo found himself at Manchester with the Drewett family. While his brothers went to Manchester Grammar School Sri Aurobindo was privately coached by Mr and Mrs Drewett. Evidently he showed even at that early age a keen proclivity towards classical languages, and Drewett grounded him well in Latin. In 1885 the Drewetts had to leave for Australia, and Sri Aurobindo was sent to St Paul's in London. The Headmaster, Dr F. W. Walker, took up Sri Aurobindo himself to ground in Greek and then pushed him rapidly into the higher classes of the school. He was at St Paul's for five years from 1884 to 1889, during which he acquired considerable proficiency in the classics and won several prizes. He also spent a good deal of his spare time in general reading 'especially English poetry, literature and fiction, French literature and the history of ancient, mediaeval and modern Europe. He spent some time also over learning Italian, some German and a little Spanish. He spent much time too in writing poetry.'[2] It is thus clear that at an early impressionable age Sri Aurobindo's keen mind was introduced to the best of classical and contemporary European culture. This explains his superb mastery over English and also the extremely broad range of his intellectual equipment.

St Paul's was a day school, and evidently the three brothers lived in London in great financial embarrassment because remittances from their father at first became irregular and then almost stopped. Thus Sri Aurobindo records that 'during a whole year a slice or two of sandwich, bread and butter and a cup of tea in the morning and in the evening a penny saveloy formed the only food'.[3]

In 1890 Sri Aurobindo won an open scholarship of £80 for

---

[1] *Sri Aurobindo on himself* p. 9. The reference to himself in the third person is due to the fact that he wrote the lines as notes while reading the manuscripts of three biographers submitted to him for correction and approval.
[2] *Sri Aurobindo on himself* p. 10.
[3] *Ibid* p. 12.

classics in his final examination at St. Paul's, and this enabled him to go on to King's College at Cambridge. He also passed his test for selection to the Indian Civil Service, standing 11th in rank and securing very high marks in classics. At Cambridge he passed the First Part of the Classics Tripos in the first division after two years, and also won college prizes for English and literary ability. He was working simultaneously for the I.C.S. examination and passed all its terminal examinations. Finally he passed the open competition with distinction, but did not qualify for the service because he did not pass the riding test. As he puts it, he 'felt no call for the I.C.S. and was seeking some way to escape from that bondage. By certain manoeuvres he managed to get himself disqualified for riding without himself rejecting the Service which his family would not have allowed him to do.'[1]

We may now try and analyse some of the political influences that had begun to impinge on the consciousness of this gifted young man, and that were so dramatically to affect his future career. It will be recalled that his father was strict in his desire that Sri Aurobindo should remain free from any Indian influence. Nevertheless, it is evident that his medical career in India had led to a sad disillusionment with the British. In fact he began sending his sons cuttings from The Bengalee newspaper in which he marked passages relating to cases of maltreatment and insult of Indians by Englishmen. In his letters he denounced the British Government in India as a heartless Government, and it seems that these communications for the first time drew Sri Aurobindo's attention and interest towards Indian politics. This interest gradually crystallized into the idea of working for the liberation of his country to which he still was, for all practical purposes, a stranger. When he went to Cambridge he came into contact there with an organization known as the Indian Majlis founded in 1891. He took an active part in the activities of the Majlis, of which he also became Secretary.[2] Along with several other hot-blooded young men he participated in its debates, and

---

[1] Sri Aurobindo on himself p. 12. This whole incident has been dealt with in detail by A. B. Purani in Sri Aurobindo in England pp. 37-78.

[2] This Society still exists, but enquiries revealed that unfortunately no minutes or records are available for the period when Sri Aurobindo was associated with it.

it seems that he delivered several speeches against British imperialism that can only be described as revolutionary. Some of the more enthusiastic young Indians at Cambridge formed a secret society romantically called 'The Lotus and Dagger' which Sri Aurobindo joined along with his brothers. Each member vowed to work for the liberation of India generally and also to take upon himself some special work to further that end. Sri Aurobindo testifies that the society was still-born, but it is nevertheless a significant incident when viewed in the context of his later contacts with secret terroristic societies in India. This much is clear; while yet at Cambridge Aurobindo had become imbued with deep patriotic fervour and a desire to dedicate himself to the liberation of his country from foreign rule. At that time of course his inspiration was exclusively European. It is very likely that he was influenced by Mazzini's *Risorgimento*. He was certainly influenced by the Irish patriotic movement that was at the time in full action. This is evident not only from his later writings when he returned to India, but also from his early poems written when he was still in England.

The writing of poetry must be considered among the noblest occupations of Man. It is generally free from any narrow selfish motive, and consists in the outpourings of the deeper and finer tendencies within the human psyche. For this reason it often mirrors the 'inner man' much more clearly than any other mode of expression, enabling the perceptive reader to look deep into the poet's inner being. As has been mentioned earlier, Sri Aurobindo started writing poetry from a very early age. Inevitably, in view of his purely European environment and education, his early poems show the deep influence of classical Greek and Latin in their allusions and names. The whole collection of his early poetry written in England was appropriately enough entitled *Songs to Myrtilla*, and is replete with classical allusions which necessarily appear rather strange and exotic to the Indian reader unacquainted with Latin and Greek. Nevertheless the poems are important, as they reveal not only Sri Aurobindo's unusual literary abilities but also his deep patriotic inclinations. In 1891 the great Irish nationalist leader Parnell died, and Sri Aurobindo wrote a short poem entitled 'Charles Steward Parnell—1891' which runs:—

'O pale and guiding light, now star unsphered,

43

Deliverer lately hailed, since by our lords
Most feared, most hated, hated because feared,
Who smot'st them with an edge surpassing swords!
Thou too wert then a child of tragic earth,
Since vainly filled thy luminous doom of birth.'

Even more explicit, and in fact foreshadowing in a remarkable
manner his future worship of India the Mother, are the following lines from 'Hic Jacet—Glasnevin Cemetery'. Addressing the
Irish nationalists he writes:—

'Patriots, behold you guerdon. This man found
Erin[1], his mother, bleeding, chastised bound,
Naked to imputation, poor, denied,
While alien masters held her house of pride.
And now behold her! Terrible and fair
With the eternal ivy in her hair,
Armed with the clamorous thunder, how she stands. . . .'

These lines graphically presage his future sorrow at seeing India
bound and bleeding under the heel of alien rulers, and his vision
of her regeneration and emancipation—sentiments which over a
decade later he expressed with unparalleled eloquence in the
pages of the Bande Mātaram and the Karmayogin. In 1896,
three years after his return to India, he wrote another, longer
poem entitled 'Lines to Ireland' which again reveal the deep
impression that the Irish national movement had made on Sri
Aurobindo's mind.

To return to Sri Aurobindo's life in England, now that he
had succeeded in getting himself disqualified from the I.C.S., a
career that in no way attracted him, he began considering
seriously returning to his motherland. Despite absence from his
native country for fourteen years, covering a most formative
period of his life from the age of seven to twenty-one, it is clear
that the deep mystical power of India was exerting its eternal
attraction on Sri Aurobindo. It so happened that an excellent
opportunity for his return soon presented itself. The late
Maharaja Sayaji Rao Gaekwar of Baroda was on a visit to
England. He was one of the most enlightened of Indian Princes,
and was well known for choosing his employees with great care
and discretion. In fact this was one of the factors which made

---

[1] A poetic form of Eire.

Baroda one of the best administered States in India. When he learned from Mr James Cotton, a son of Sir Henry Cotton, that a talented and enthusiastic young man with excellent educational qualifications was looking for a job he at once jumped at the idea. The matter was settled after a private interview which the Maharaja had with Sri Aurobindo, as the result of which the latter joined the Baroda State service and sailed for India in February 1893.

Thus ended one phase of the career of this remarkable man, and another opened which was destined to transform him into a fiery apostle of spiritual Nationalism and to catapult him into the very centre of the political scene in India. It is of interest to review his attainments when he set sail for India. Having spent fourteen years in England he had acquired, as we have seen, a mastery over English and French—the two greatest contemporary European languages, as well as Latin and Greek—the two great classical European languages. He had also acquired some familiarity with German and Italian, and had shown literary ability of a high order. In addition to these impressive accomplishments he had revealed deep poetical sensibility, and had also been deeply affected by nationalistic fervour, specially by the Irish movement against British rule. The fire of patriotism was already burning within him, and had created in him a firm resolve to work for his country's liberation. This combination of intellectual ability, artistic sensibility and patriotic fervour required only the deep spiritualizing influence of India—with her age-old philosophy and culture stretching back unbroken into the dawn of history—to transform Sri Aurobindo into one of the most remarkable political figures in the history of modern India.

4

RETURN TO INDIA IN 1893

THE BARODA PERIOD

IN 1893, after staying abroad for over fourteen years, Sri Aurobindo returned to India and proceeded to Baroda to take up
service in that State. He continued in service there for over
thirteen years right up to 1907, though in the later years he
often took long leaves of absence to attend to nationalistic
activity. Finally the pressure of national events forced him to
resign and jump into the very midst of active politics in Bengal,
which was in turmoil as the result of Lord Curzon's partition of
that Province in 1905. The period 1893-1905 can thus be considered a preparatory phase for Sri Aurobindo's short but
meteoric career of active politics, which culminated in his
equally dramatic withdrawal in 1910. In this chapter it is
proposed to study the early development of his political thought
during the Baroda period.

On first joining Baroda State Service Sri Aurobindo was put
in the Settlement Department in order to familiarize himself
with various aspects of the work there; then in the Stamps &
Revenue Departments; then in the Secretariat for drawing up
despatches and other documents. His first teaching assignment
was when his services were lent to the Baroda College to give
French lessons for certain periods in the week. Other college
work was gradually added and finally the College Principal
requested the Maharaja to appoint him to the permanent post of
Professor of English. To this the Maharaja agreed in 1900 and
Sri Aurobindo rose to become the Vice-Principal of the College
and once acted as Principal also. In the meantime the Maharaja,
whenever he thought fit, would send for Sri Aurobindo to
assist him in writing letters, composing speeches or drawing up
documents that required special phrasing ability such as letters
and minutes to the Government of India.[1] It seems that the

Maharaja also asked Sri Aurobindo to tutor his children, probably in English.[2] He accompanied the Maharaja to Naini Tal and also to Kashmir, during which visits he acted virtually as his private secretary. But it appears that he was temperamentally unsuited to life at the court of a Prince, however enlightened, and there was a good deal of friction between them. Thereafter his contacts with the Maharaja were mainly informal and on an *ad hoc* basis.

It will be recalled that for the fourteen years immediately preceding his arrival in Baroda, from 1879 to 1893, Sri Aurobindo had lived and studied in England. The seven years prior to that were also spent in a most un-Indian setting, as the whole atmosphere of his father's house was far from national. As we saw in the previous chapter, his only contact with Indian thought and conditions while in England was contacts with some Indian students, association with the Indian Majlis at Cambridge, perusal of some newspaper cuttings sent to him occasionally by his father, and a rather perfunctory study of Bengali after passing the I.C.S. competitive examination. In this context it is all the more remarkable that almost immediately after he took up service in Baroda he launched a series of articles that are distinguished not only for their literary qualities but for the deep awareness of Indian history, culture and contemporary conditions that they reveal. Before proceeding with a study of his early writings, however, it will be helpful to take note of his spiritual interests and inclinations which form the bedrock alike of his literary work as of his political philosophy. In fact it would not be incorrect to say that Sri Aurobindo's political theory was firmly grounded in and grew out of his deep spiritual convictions. Politics for him were an extension, as it were, of his theory of personal, national and universal spiritual development. As we will see later, the spiritual element in Sri Aurobindo's thought increasingly predominated, until in

[1] e.g. Memorandum on Imperial Service troops dated August 1, 1904, in reply to a letter on the subject addressed to the Maharaja by Lord Curzon a few months earlier. (Vide Records of Baroda Government—Scheme for Reorganization of the Baroda State Forces, Volume II).

[2] This information was given to me by the Maharaja's only daughter, who is now the dowager Maharani of Cooch-Behar. She said that Sri Aurobindo used to come to teach her and her brothers, and recalls that they used often to play truant because he was too immersed in thoughts and idealistic dreamings really to pay much attention to them.

1910 it compelled him to depart dramatically from the scene of active politics so that he could give his full attention to his spiritual adventure.

Immediately upon settling down in Baroda Sri Aurobindo plunged into the study of Indian languages, culture, history and religion. He was, it must be remembered, an accomplished scholar in the Western tradition, having attained proficiency in Latin, Greek and French as well as a fair acquaintance with Italian and German. His command over English was, of course, exceptional and revealed itself in his masterly and poetical style. Thus he approached Indian philosophy with a mind already sharpened by contact with the best that Western culture had to offer and free from the narrow, parochial and dogmatic outlook which so many educated Indians at that time displayed. This intellectual equipment helped him greatly in his study of Indian thought and literature, and within a short time he was studying from the classics of Hindu philosophy. He also learnt Bengali and was deeply impressed by the writings of Bankim Chandra Chatterjee, the great Bengali novelist, and Michael Madhusudan Dutt, the pioneer in modern Bengali poetry.[1]

This study at the fountainhead of Indian philosophy made a deep impression upon Sri Aurobindo's mind, already richly dyed in the Western intellectual tradition. The message of the great Hindu classics, however, is not purely or even predominantly directed towards the intellect. It goes much deeper, appealing to the very inmost centre of a person's being. It is evident that Sri Aurobindo must have been so affected, for his subsequent writings reveal that the impact had reached far beyond the merely intellectual level. The crux of Hindu philosophy is that the all-pervasive spiritual Reality is to be actively and consciously realized and experienced. A mere intellectual exposi-

[1] In his seven articles in the Indu Prakash on Bankim Chandra Chatterjee, published in 1894, he pays a moving and eloquent tribute to the great novelist, and also in passing to the great poet Dutt. Concluding the series, he writes:

'And when posterity comes to crown with her praises the makers of India, she will place her most splendid laurel not on the sweating temples of a place-hunting politician nor on the narrow forehead of a noisy social reformer but on the serene brow of that gracious Bengali (Bankim) who never clamoured for place or power, but did his work in silence for love of his work, even as nature does, and, just because he had no aim but to give out the best that was in him, was able to create a language, a literature and a nation.'

tion of the various systems of philosophy is in itself futile and pointless. Any serious student of Hinduism is, therefore, inexorably led on towards undertaking spiritual practices, of which there is a wide range of choice, in the hope that the lead of his merely intellectual knowledge will be transmuted into the gold of realization. This process is clearly revealed in the case of Sri Aurobindo. His study of the Hindu classics led him in 1904[1] to take up some spiritual practices, which in turn strengthened his intellectual predilections towards religion.

Sri Aurobindo's biographies[2] tell us that his first distinct spiritual 'experience' was in 1893 immediately upon landing by the steamer 'Carthage' at Bombay, an experience of infinite calm descending upon him as soon as he set foot upon his native soil after an absence of over fourteen years. Again, during a driving incident in 1901, some divine figure seemed to come out of his body and saved him from an accident to his carriage. In 1903 during a visit to Kashmir he had another important spiritual experience of being in the midst of the 'Vacant Infinite' while walking on the Shankaracharya Hill. It is of course neither possible nor necessary here to discuss the objective validity of these experiences. Suffice it to say that for him they were valid, and they are mentioned to indicate the importance that the spiritual aspect had assumed for him even during his stay at Baroda.

At first Sri Aurobindo did not connect his experiences with Yoga, and in fact when his friend Shri K. G. Deshpande once asked him to take up the practice of Yoga he refused to do so. Gradually, however, the urgency of the call deepened, until it ultimately became an insistent demand which could not be resisted.[3] Although he was not able to find a Guru to suit him, he did obtain inspiration from several people, and later some

---

[1] *On himself and the Mother* p. 37.
[2] e.g. *Mahayogi* by Shri R. R. Diwakar.
[3] The following extract from a letter to his wife dated August 30, 1905, is revealing:
'I must have direct perception of God through whatever means possible...
If there is a God, there must be a way to have spiritual contact with Him. That way may be very tortuous and difficult, full of dangers, but I am firmly resolved to follow that path. Hinduism says that the path lies in one's body, in one's soul. I am following the rules prescribed for following that path. Even in the course of one month I am feeling that the words of Hinduism are not false. I am experiencing all the beatific marks of which Hinduism speaks. Now I wish I could also take you through the same path.'

D

concrete guidance from one Shri Lele of Gwalior.[1] Thus at Baroda his life flowed in two complementary streams, his visible Government career and activities, and the deeper, more fundamental, spiritual current which, though not visible at the surface, yet profoundly shaped and influenced his general philosophy of life as well as his political thought.

Sri Aurobindo's first political writings were a series of articles begun in 1893 entitled 'New Lamps for Old'[2] written at the instance of his Cambridge friend Shri K. G. Deshpande who edited the English section of an Anglo-Marathi paper known as the *Indu Prakash*. The first two articles in the series created a sensation among the intelligentsia, as they constituted a direct, incisive and eloquent attack on the policies adopted by the Indian National Congress and a stirring call to his countrymen to shake off the torpor of centuries and to arise to liberate their Motherland. It is said that the great liberal leader Mahadev Govind Ranade warned the proprietor of the *Indu Prakash* that if the series were continued in the same tone he would run a grave risk of prosecution for sedition. The original plan of 'New Lamps for Old' had thus to be abandoned at the instance of the proprietor. The Editor, however, requested Sri Aurobindo to continue the series in a modified tone. This he reluctantly consented to do and he wrote in all eleven articles, the last being dated March 6, 1894.[3] His being in State service prevented him from publicly acknowledging his writings, and the articles were published anonymously. He also published anonymously in the

[1] Aurobindo met Vishnu Bhaskar Lele in 1907 after the Surat Congress. His brother Barindra writes that it was he (Barindra) who brought the two together in Baroda. According to Barindra Shri Lele did not believe in the cult of 'Purification by blood and fire'. (cf. *Atmacharit* by Barindra Kumar Ghose p. 40). Barindra reports that Sri Aurobindo went to see Swami Brahmananda in 1903. The Swami used to live at Chando on the Narmada. Barindra further reports that the Swami looked at Aurobindo and Aurobindo had spiritual experiences. He writes 'This must have been the first real spiritual touch which was destined in the time to open Aurobindo's being to Higher Truths.'

[2] 'This title did not refer to Indian civilization but to Congress politics. It is not used in the sense of the Aladdin story, but was intended to imply the offering of new lights to replace the old and faint reformist lights of the Congress' (*On himself and the Mother*) p. 27.

[3] Nine articles are published in *Sri Aurobindo's Political Thought* by Professors Haridas & Uma Mukherjee—pp. 61-123. Two articles, numbers 9 and 10, have still not been traced.

Indu Prakash, from July 16th to August 27, 1894, seven articles upon Bankim Chandra Chatterjee,[1] which are valuable for the light they throw on the working of his mind in the early Baroda period.

A close study of the *Indu Prakash* articles and also other evidence reveals three distinct strands in Sri Aurobindo's early political thought—Sri Aurobindo as a critic of the Congress; as a critic of the British; and his positive programme of political action. As his early thought contains the seeds of his later elaborations, these aspects deserve detailed consideration.

Sri Aurobindo as a critic of the Congress

From the very first line he wrote upon political affairs in 1893, right up to his withdrawal from active politics in 1910, Sri Aurobindo was a trenchant critic of the Congress. This does not mean, of course, that the formation of that organization did not at first thrill him deeply. In his very first article[2] he recalls this when he writes 'How shall we find words vivid enough to describe the fervour of those morning hopes, the April splendour of that wonderful enthusiasm? The Congress was to us all that is to man most dear, most high, and most sacred; a well of living water in deserts more than Saharan; a proud banner in the battle of liberty and a holy temple of concord where the races met and mingled.' But these hopes were utterly belied, and in his early writings Sri Aurobindo indicts the Congress on at least four distinct counts.

To begin with he felt that the Congress leaders did not adopt a clear-cut goal of national freedom, but instead wasted its time on immaterial trifles which could not at all meet the requirements of the situation. As the result, all that the Congress had been able to achieve since its inception were a few paltry administrative reforms which he contemptuously compares to cheap conjuring tricks. He writes 'I say of the Congress, then, this—that its aims are mistaken, that the spirit in which it proceeds towards their accomplishment is not a spirit of sincerity and whole-heartedness, and that the methods it has chosen are not the right methods, and the leaders in whom it trusts not the

[1] Published under the title *Bankim Chandra Chatterjee* by Sri Aurobindo Ashrama, Pondicherry.
[2] New Lamps for Old No. 1, *Indu Prakash* August 7, 1893.

right sort of men to be leaders;—in brief, that we are at present the blind led, if not by the blind, at any rate by the one-eyed."[1]

Secondly, Sri Aurobindo felt that even for the achievement of its shamefully modest demands the Congress adopted the wrong approach towards the British. Instead of relying on the inherent strength of the nation, it sought by flattery to gain the good-will of its foreign rulers.[2] He says 'There was a little too much talk about the blessings of British rule, and the inscrutable Providence which has laid us in the maternal, or more properly the step-maternal, bosom of just and benevolent England. Yet more appalling was the general timidity of the Congress, its glossing over of hard names, its disinclination to tell the direct truth, its fear of too deeply displeasing our masters.[3]

Thirdly, he strongly criticized the Congress creed that gradual political development, or 'widening progress', as they put it, was the inevitable law in all ages and all countries and must necessarily be followed in India. Bringing close historical analysis to bear on the problem he showed that this emphatic-ally has not been the case in France, Ireland and many other countries. Significantly, he wrote 'Rather we know that the first step of that fortunate country (France) towards progress was not through any decent and orderly expansion, but through purification by blood and fire. It was not a convocation of res-pectable citizens, but the vast and ignorant proletariat, that emerged from a prolonged and almost coeval apathy and blotted out in five terrible years the accumulated oppression of thirteen centuries.'[4]

Perhaps Sri Aurobindo's strongest indictment of the Con-gress, however, was the charge that instead of evoking and organizing the support of the vast Indian proletariat it remained a closely restricted middle-class organization, or, as he puts it 'a middle-class organ, selfish and disingenuous in its public action and hollow in its professions of a large and disinterested patriotism.[5] He lamented the fact that the Congress had fallen

[1] New Lamps for Old No. 3, *Indu Prakash* August 28, 1893.

[2] Thus, in one of his articles on Bankim, he satirically calls the organiza-tion the 'Indian Unnational Congress'—'B. C. Chatterjee', p. 46.

[3] New Lamps for Old No. 4, *Indu Prakash*, August 7, 1893.

[4] *Ibid* No. 4, *Indu Prakash*, September 18, 1893.

[5] New Lamps for Old No. 7, *Indu Prakash*, December 4, 1893. The follow-ing extract from the Congress speech of Sir Pherozshah Mehta in 1900 well illustrates the attitude of paternal and supercilious benevolence which the

so far short of the immense possibilities that lay before it, and
he took the Congress leaders severely to task for this. His clear
recognition of the vital necessity of converting the national
movement into a mass of movement incorporating the Indian
proletariat is well illustrated in the following extracts from his
early writings, which combine devastating sarcasm with a profound awareness of the prime necessity of mass awakening and
participation in the national movement:

". . . Mr Pherozshah, in the generous heat of his temperate
and carefully restricted patriotism, assures us after his genial
manner that the awakening of the masses from their ignorance
and misery is entirely unimportant and any expenditure of
energy in that direction is entirely premature. . . . But with
that distressed and ignorant proletariat—now that the middle
class has proved deficient in sincerity, power and judgment—
with that proletariat resides, whether we like it or not, our sole
assurance of hope, our sole chance in the future. . . . Theorist
and trifler though I may be called, I again assert as our first and
holiest duty the elevation and enlightenment of the proletariat.'[1]

And again:

'Yet the proletariat is, as I have striven to show, the real key of
the situation. Torpid he is and immobile; he is nothing of an
actual force, but he is a very great potential force, and whoever
succeeds in understanding and eliciting his strength, becomes
by the very fact master of the future. Our situation is indeed
complex and difficult beyond any that has ever been imagined
by the human intellect; but if there is one thing clear in it, it is
that the right and fruitful policy for the burgess, the only policy
that has any chance of eventual success, is to base his cause
upon the adroit management of the proletariat. He must awaken
and organize the entire power of the country and thus multiply
infinitely his volume and significance, the better to attain
supremacy as much social as political.'[2]

Moderate leaders adopted towards the masses and which was so eloquently
attacked by Sri Aurobindo.

"If the masses were capable of giving articulate expression to definite
political demands, then the time would have arrived not for consultative
councils but for representative institutions . . . it is because they are
unable to do so that the function and the duty devolve upon their educated
and enlightened compatriots to feel, to understand and to interpret their
grievances.'

[1] *Ibid* No. 7, *Indu Prakash*, December 4, 1893.

[2] New Lamps for Old No. 11, *Indu Prakash*, March 6, 1894.

This clear, unambiguous declaration is particularly significant in view of the fact that one of the main achievements of the Radical party a few years later was in fact to enthuse the masses with the idea of freedom, and for the first time to give the national movement a mass character.

Sri Aurobindo as a critic of the British

Every person who participated in the struggle for India's national liberation was of necessity a critic of her foreign masters. Until Sri Aurobindo's advent, however, this criticism had been indirect, muted and heavily camouflaged so as not to incur the wrath of the British. Sri Aurobindo's articles in the *Indu Prakash* marked a completely new departure from the existing practice and contained a direct and eloquent attack upon the British which, as we have mentioned, caused a considerable sensation in the country. It is clear that his object in doing so was twofold; to strengthen the anti-British sentiment in the country and to break the myth of British superiority and the almost superstitious view widely held at the time that they were demi-gods whose greatness was unassailable.

Sri Aurobindo's criticism was in two directions. Firstly, by elaborate historical analysis, he sought to show that the British political organization and system was by no means the best that the West had to offer. While he accepted the necessity of admitting into India Occidental ideas, methods and culture, he was emphatic that it must choose only that which is best in Western modes of thought and organization and by no means swallow wholesale whatever Britain might try and force down its throat. This, incidentally, reveals clearly that Sri Aurobindo was by no means obscurantist or narrowly revivalistic in his approach to the problem of Indian political development. In some very interesting analysis he compares the British system of socio-political organization to the continental, specially the French. Though he admits that the weakness of the latter is its inability to create firm and stable political institutions, he indicts the former for laying too much stress on mere institutionalism while ignoring the vitally important factor of social freedom and equality. He concludes the analysis by saying:

'We in India, or at any rate those races among us which are in the van of every forward movement, are far more nearly allied

54

to the French and Athenian than to the Anglo-Saxon, but owing to the accident of British domination our intellects have been carefully nurtured on a purely English diet. Hence we do not care to purchase an outfit of political ideas properly adjusted to our natural temper and urgent requirements, but must eke out our scanty wardrobe with the cast-off rags and threadbare leavings of our English masters . . .'[1]

Such fundamental sociological criticism of the British, based on careful historical analysis, was something entirely new to the Indian scene at the time Sri Aurobindo wrote, and had a deep impact upon the English-educated intelligentsia in the country.

The second, more obvious, direction of Sri Aurobindo's criticism was towards British policies in India and the behaviour of their officials. The former had led to the stifling of the Indian spirit, the cramping of her potentialities for development, and her economic ruin. This is clearly implied in all his writings, and often explicitly stated, for example when he writes that '. . . the dark spectre of Penury draws her robe over the land in greater volume and with an ampler sweep.'[2] Regarding the British officials in India, he is merciless with his satire. He writes:

'I grant that they are rude and arrogant, that they govern badly, that they are devoid of any great or generous emotion, that their conduct is that of a small coterie of masters surrounded by a nation of Helots. But to say all this is simply to say that they are very common place men put into a quite unique position. They are really ordinary men—and not only ordinary men, but ordinary Englishmen—types of the middle-class or Philistines, in the graphic English phrase, with the narrow hearts and commercial habit of mind peculiar to that sort of people.'[3]

Sri Aurobindo is no less severe in his criticism of the system of administration which the British had set up in India, which he felt was thoroughly unsuited to Indian conditions and the natural genius of the Indian people. Writing about the educational system, for example, he says.

'. . . our system of public instruction, the most ingeniously

---

[1] New Lamps for Old No. 5, *Indu Prakash*, October 30, 1893.
[2] *Ibid*, No. 1, *Indu Prakash*, August 7, 1893.
[3] *Ibid* No. 2, *Indu Prakash*, August 21, 1893.

complete machine for murder that human stupidity ever invented, and murder not only of a man's body but of a man's soul, of that sacred fire of individuality in him which is far holier and more precious than this mere mortal breath.'[1]

In addition to criticizing British officialdom and their policies in India, Sri Aurobindo was merciless in his contempt for the Indians who were 'servilely English'. He poured scorn upon 'The Anglicized Babu (who) sits in the high place and rules the earth for a season. It is he who perorates on the Congress, who frolics in the abysmal fatuity of interpellation on the Legislative Council, who mismanages civic affairs in the smile of the City Corporation. He is the man of the present, but he is not the man of the future.'[2]

Sri Aurobindo's positive programme of political action.

So far we have been considering Sri Aurobindo's political thought as a critique both of the current policies and leadership of the Congress and also of the British. Now we will turn to the more positive aspect of his political theory as it emerges in his early Baroda period. Later, from 1905-1910, when he entered actively the political fray, Sri Aurobindo dealt much more exhaustively with the technique of political action against the British. Even in the Baroda period, however, it is clear that the broad contours of his future policy were gradually beginning to form in his mind. This aspect of his thought may be studied from two aspects, his theoretical approach to the problem of Indian freedom and the concrete measures whereby he envisaged this could be brought about.

His theoretical approach can be summed up by saying that his goal for India was complete freedom from British domination, and that for this emancipation she must rely not on the charity or condescension of her foreign masters but on her own limitless reservoir of inner strength and power. In one of his early articles appears the following eloquent passage which well illustrates this point:

'Our actual enemy is not any force exterior to ourselves, but our

---

[1] 'Bankim Chandra Chatterjee' (Sri Aurobindo), p. 26.
[2] Ibid pp. 44-45.
[3] New Lamps for Old No. 2, Indu Prakash, August 21, 1893.

own crying weaknesses, our cowardice, our selfishness, our hypocrisy, our purblind sentimentalism. I really cannot see why we should rage so furiously against the Anglo-Indians[1] and call them by all manner of opprobrious epithets. . . . It is something very like folly to quarrel with them for not transgressing the law of their own nature.[2] If we were not dazzled by the artificial glare of English prestige, we should at once acknowledge that these men are really not worth being angry with: and if it is idle to be angry with them, it is still more unprofitable to rate their opinion of us at more than a straw's value. Our appeal, the appeal of every high-souled and self-respecting nation, ought not to lie to the opinion of the Anglo-Indians, no, nor yet to the British sense of justice, but to our own reviving sense of manhood, to our own sincere fellow-feeling—so far as it can be called sincere—with the silent and suffering people of India. I am sure that eventually the nobler part of us will prevail—that when we no longer obey the dictates of a veiled self-interest, but return to the profession of a large and genuine patriotism, when we cease to hanker after the soiled crumbs which England may cast to us from her table, then it will be to that sense of manhood, to that sincere fellow-feeling that we shall finally and forcibly appeal.'

Coming as it did from a young man who was at the time only twenty-one years old and had just returned to his homeland after an absence of over fourteen years, this passage not only reveals remarkable maturity and power of expression but also shows that the broad contours of Sri Aurobindo's approach to Indian emancipation were already clearly formed in his mind even at this early stage. It is evident that throughout his stay at Baroda he was revolving in his mind how best he could contribute towards liberating his motherland from its foreign yoke, and by the time the partition of Bengal came in 1905 as a god-sent opportunity he had carefully thought over and discussed with some of his intimate friends the best line of action to adopt.

When in England, Sri Aurobindo had already decided to devote his life to the service of his country and its liberation. It was in pursuance of this objective that he began writing on political matters soon after his return to India, trying to awaken

[1] i.e. English officials governing in India. At that time the term was not used in its present racial sense.
[2] i.e. their *Swadharma*, an important philosophical concept expounded in the *Bhagwadgita*.

the nation to his ideas and approach to the problem of Indian freedom. But as these were not well received by the leaders of the time he drew back temporarily into silence, without how-ever abandoning either his ideas or his hope for effective political action.[1] In his own words, though he refers to himself in the third person, there were three sides to his political ideas and activities—'First, there was the action with which he started, a secret revolutionary propaganda and organization of which the central object was the preparation of an armed insurrection. Secondly, there was a public propaganda intended to convert the whole nation to the ideal of independence which was re-garded, when he entered into politics, by the vast majority of Indians as unpractical and impossible, an almost insane chimera. It was thought that the British Empire was too powerful and India too weak, effectively disarmed and impotent even to dream of the success of such an endeavour. Thirdly, there was the organization of the people to carry on a public and united opposition and undermining of the foreign rule through an in-creasing non-co-operation and passive resistance.'[2]

The first active step taken by Sri Aurobindo, apart from the *Indu Prakash* articles, was to send a young Bengali soldier of the Baroda army, one Jatin Banerjee, to Bengal with the object of establishing secretly groups which would undertake revolu-tionary propaganda and recruitment throughout that province. Jatin succeeded in forming the first group in Calcutta, and also entered into relations with P. Mitter and other revolutionaries in other parts of Bengal. He was joined later by Barindra Ghosh, Sri Aurobindo's younger brother. Lizelle Raymond, in her fascinating biography of Sister Nivedita, says:

'Barindra's work in Bengal was the organization in the villages —even the most remote—of a chain of Samitis, or youth organizations, which would meet under all kinds of pretexts, but with the real aim of providing a civic and political education and opening the eyes of the young to the "affairs of the nation". Similar youth organizations had already been established in the Deccan under the leadership of the outspoken nationalist leader Bal Gangadrha Tilak. In smoky little grain shops, on the terraced roofs of private houses, young men would meet to hear about

[1] *On Himself and the Mother* (Sri Aurobindo) p. 26.
[2] *Ibid*, p. 38.

the lives of Mazzini and Garibaldi, to read exhortations from
Swami Vivekananda, to listen to the warlike incidents of the
Mahabharata and to comments on the *Bhagwad Gita*. The
number of samitis increased daily.'[1]

In the meantime Sri Aurobindo had contacted and become a
member of a Secret Society in Western India, and had been introduced to its Council in Bombay. In fact he brought about a
sort of liaison between this Society, which was headed by a
prominent Rajput noble of Udaipur, and the revolutionary
group in Bengal led by P. Mitter.[2] The modus operandi was to
be the setting up of Societies of young men, ostensibly for
physical, cultural and intellectual activities, who were secretly
to be trained in the technique of revolutionary action. Although
Sri Aurobindo's attempt to bring about a close organization of
the whole movement did not succeed, the general idea was taken
up by many separate groups throughout the country.[3]

Sister Nivedita, the Irish disciple of Swami Vivekananda, was
among the few persons in India who knew that Sri Aurobindo
was the directing brain behind the nationalist movement in
Bengal, despite his physical absence. As her biographer, Lizelle
Raymond, writes:

'In this India a spontaneous enthusiasm, born of the country's
own needs, was necessary before the revolutionary movement
could be properly formed, and for that, consciously or unconsciously, all eyes were turned towards Aurobindo Ghosh. The
plan which he envisaged and on which he was working could
be revealed only to minds in a fit state to receive it.'[4]

The same author gives us the valuable information that
Nivedita was 'one of the five members of the political committee
which Aurobindo Ghosh had appointed in Bengal to unite in a
single organization the small and scattered groups of rebels
which had sprung into existence and were acting without reference to one another. The other members were P. Mitter, a
lawyer and revolutionary leader, Jatin Banerjee, C. R. Das and
Surendranath Tagore. Until the time when Aurobindo Ghosh

---

[1] *The Dedicated*, by Lizelle Raymond, pp. 283-84.
[2] *On Himself and the Mother* (Sri Aurobindo), pp. 28 and 42.
[3] *Ibid*, p. 43.
[4] *The Dedicated*, by Lizelle Raymond, p. 282.

himself came to settle in Bengal in 1905, the committee was only intermittently successful in its liaison work, but it did enlist tens of thousands of young men in the nationalist movement, and created a living body of young pioneers of Indian independence.'[1] This clearly reveals that even during his stay in Baroda Sri Aurobindo had been accepted as the intellectual leader of the revolutionary movement in Bengal.

The rationale of this revolutionary activity at the time is well expressed by Sri Aurobindo in the following extract from notes and letters on his life:

'At that time the military organization of the great empires and their means of military action were not so overwhelming and apparently irresistible as they now are: the rifle was still the decisive weapon, air power had not yet been developed and the force of artillery was not so devastating as it afterwards became. India was disarmed, but Sri Aurobindo thought that with proper organization and help from outside this difficulty might be overcome and in so vast a country as India and with the smallness of the regular British armies, even a guerrilla warfare accompanied by general resistance and revolt might be effective. There was also the possibility of a general revolt in the Indian army. At the same time he had studied the temperament and characteristics of the British people and the turn of their political instincts, and he believed that although they would resist any attempt at self-liberation by the Indian people and would at the most only concede very slowly such reforms as would not weaken their imperial control, still they were not of the kind which would be ruthlessly adamantine to the end: if they found resistance and revolt becoming general and persistent they would in the end try to arrive at an accommodation to save what they could of their empire or in an extremity prefer to grant independence rather than have it forcefully wrested from their hands.'[2]

It may be mentioned that one of the ablest men in these revolutionary groups was a Marhatta named Sakharam Ganesh Deuskar whose family had long been domiciled in Bengal. In his popular life of Shivaji in Bengali he first brought in the term 'Swaraj'. He also published a book entitled *Desher Katha* describing in exhaustive detail the commercial and industrial

[1] *Ibid*, p. 296.
[2] *On Himself and the Mother* (Sri. Aurobindo), pp. 38-39.

exploitation of India by the British. This book had an immense repercussion in Bengal and captured the imagination of young Bengalis. It also strengthened Sri Aurobindo's view that shaking off the British economic yoke and the parallel development of Indian trade and industry was a necessary concomitant of the revolutionary endeavour.[1]

We learn that Sri Aurobindo included very early in the scope of his revolutionary work an activity that later became an important item in the public programme of the nationalist party, Swadeshi, or economic self-sufficiency through indigenous industry. Though at that time the idea was still in its infancy and was considered a fad of the few, he encouraged young men in the revolutionary centres to propagate the Swadeshi creed.[2]

Thus we see that in the absence of any political party openly wedded to the idea of Indian freedom, Sri Aurobindo actively plunged into secret revolutionary activity. Later, when the partition of Bengal brought an extremist party into the open as the spearhead of a great nationalist movement, his activities turned more and more in the direction of party activity and the secret action became a secondary and subordinate element.[3] At no time, however, did he reject the use of force as and when necessary in order to bring about the emancipation of the motherland from foreign domination. This aspect of his thought is discussed in greater detail later in this work.

[1] *On Himself and the Mother* (Sri Aurobindo), p. 46.
[2] *Ibid*, p. 45.
[3] *Ibid*, p. 43.

5

THE CRISIS OF 1905 AND THE RISE OF RADICALISM

In the previous chapter we reviewed Sri Aurobindo's political ideas while in Baroda. It is clear that he was looking and waiting for the best opportunity to serve the cause of his country's freedom. Before 1905, however, the time for his active participation in politics was not ripe. As one of his biographers puts it, 'Meanwhile the "mendicant" policy of the "moderates" continued as the official policy of the Indian National Congress; the political pulse of the nation was below par; his own province of Bengal—anything but intrepid at the time—was in no mood to be persuaded by Sri Aurobindo and his gospel of virile nationalism. He decided therefore to ply the pedagogic furrow for yet a while longer, till Bengal and the country as a whole should be willing and ready to receive and translate into action his militant nationalist programme'.[1] As we have seen, however, his political activities at Baroda were by no means merely academic. In the absence of any party prepared openly to advocate a policy of bold nationalism, Sri Aurobindo turned his attention towards secret revolutionary action.

In 1905, however, there occurred an event which at once galvanized the nation into a mood peculiarly suitable for the spread of radical ideas and caused a mass upsurge of resentment against the British. Lord Curzon, that gifted though vain and obstinate Viceroy of India, decided in the teeth of opposition from the Bengalis to partition the Province of Bengal. Almost overnight the ground was cut from under the feet of the Moderates, and mass opinion—not only in Bengal but in other parts of India such as Maharashtra and the Punjab where political consciousness was well developed—veered strongly in favour of the nationalist creed. In one of his speeches delivered

[1] *Sri Aurobindo* (Iyengar), p. 106.

in 1908 Sri Aurobindo graphically describes how the Bengal partition jolted the nation into a new awareness of its true nature. He says:

'We in India fell under the influence of the foreigners' *Maya*[1] which completely possessed our souls. It was the *Maya* of the alien rule, the alien civilization, the powers and capacities of the alien people who happen to rule over us. These were as if so many shackles that put our physical, intellectual and moral life into bondage. We went to school with the aliens, we allowed the aliens to teach us and draw our minds away from all that was great and good in us. We considered ourselves unfit for self-Government and political life, we looked to England as our exemplar and took her as our saviour. And all this was *Maya* and bondage. . . . It is only through repression and suffering that this *Maya* can be dispelled and the bitter fruit of partition of Bengal administered by Lord Curzon dispelled the illusion. We looked up and saw that the brilliant bird sitting above was none else but ourselves, our real and actual self.[2] Thus we found *Swaraj*[3] within ourselves and saw that it was in our hands to discover and to realize it.'[4]

This was the opportunity for which Sri Aurobindo and those who thought like him were waiting. They plunged into furious political activity which, within the course of five short years, changed the entire complexion of Indian politics and set in motion a chain of events that within four decades resulted in India emerging as an independent nation.

The partition of Bengal became a legal fact on September 29, 1905. The whole province was seething with resentment. Early

[1] Illusion, an important term in Indian monistic philosophy.

[2] The allusion is to the celebrated parable of the two birds in the *Katha Upanishada*.

[3] Self-government.

[4] *Speeches* (Sri Aurobindo), pp. 36-37. It may be added that the Moderate wing of the Congress received the partition with undisguised dismay, because they realized that it completely cut the ground from under their feet and gave a tremendous boost to their rivals the Radicals. Thus, in his undelivered Presidential Address of 1907, Rash Behari Ghosh makes a scathing indictment against Lord Curzon for his policies. After many charges he says: 'And, lastly, we charge him with having set Bengal in a blaze. It is Lord Curzon and Lord Curzon alone who is responsible for the rise of the new party, for he drove the people to despair and to madness.'

in 1906, on March 12th, a weekly journal in English entitled *Yugantar* was started in Calcutta by Barindra Ghosh, Sri Aurobindo's fiery younger brother. To this Sri Aurobindo was a frequent contributor, though as he was still in Baroda service his name did not appear. On April 14th he attended the political conference in Barisal, which was broken up by a police lathi charge. In the middle of 1906 he took one year's leave from the Baroda College without pay and proceeded to Calcutta where he actively plunged into the task of organizing the nationalist movement in Bengal. On August 6th Bipin Chandra Pal started an English Weekly called *Bande Mātaram*. He asked Sri Aurobindo to join him in this venture, to which he readily agreed as he saw in this an excellent opportunity for starting the public propaganda necessary for his revolutionary purpose. It was in this journal, as well as in the *Karmayogin* which Sri Aurobindo started in the middle of 1909, that we find copious material from which emerges his political philosophy.

It is proposed to deal with his political thought, as it emerges during the crucial period 1905-1910, in two broad categories. First we shall examine the philosophical basis of his political theory, and the clear goal of political endeavour which flows logically therefrom. Next, we shall study in detail the technique and tactics of political action which he expounded for the achievement of this goal. Both aspects are important, because Sri Aurobindo was at once a profound political theorist as well as a shrewd political tactician—a combination of talents only too rare in history.

PART III

THE PHILOSOPHICAL BASIS OF SRI AUROBINDO'S THOUGHT, AND HIS POLITICAL GOAL

6

SRI AUROBINDO AS AN IDEALIST—HIS THEORY OF SPIRITUAL EVOLUTION

THE great thinkers of the world fall within two basic categories of thought, the Idealistic and the Materialistic. Most Indian Philosophers have been Idealists and this applies to Sri Aurobindo also, although as we shall see his philosophy contains some original aspects not to be found in the traditional Hindu systems of thought. While his general philosophical system was finalized and perfected at Pondicherry after his active political career, it is clear that its contours began gradually shaping in his mind ever since he returned from England, and that it deeply influenced his political thinking. It may therefore be helpful to give a brief outline of his philosophy in as simple terms as possible. Sri Aurobindo has coined numerous technical terms to express his philosophical concepts, but in the following analysis these have been avoided wherever possible.

As we have said, Sri Aurobindo was an Idealist. He writes:

'According to our philosophy it is the idea which expresses itself in matter and takes to itself bodies. This is true also in the life of Humanity; it is true in politics, in the progress and life of a nation. It is the idea which shapes material institutions.'[1]

This is of course an ancient concept, established in the West by Plato and held in India for many centuries before that by the Vedic seers. But Sri Aurobindo gives it a peculiar significance in his theory of spiritual evolution. According to this theory, creation began when a part of the Supreme, Unconditioned and Absolute Reality plunged into the grossest and densest matter. From that dawn of creation the Spirit that was involved in matter began its slow but sure evolution on the path which leads back to its source of origin. After aeons, life began to

---

[1] *Speeches* (Sri Aurobindo), p. 91.

make its appearance in primitive forms which gradually evolved upwards. Then, after another tremendous gap, mind first appeared among living creatures. The next step upwards was the advent of the human race when intellect began to assume the dominating role. This, however, is by no means the final phase of evolution. In fact it is an intermediate stage, and mankind is now poised on the threshold of the next leap forward in the evolutionary process. This step is the evolution of mind to Supermind, the luminous realm of Truth-Consciousness, which will be a development even more profound than the preceding step from animal to human consciousness. The instruments of this Supermind will be intuition and direct cognition rather than the imperfect reasoning intellect which our race possesses at present.

There is one great difference, however, between the previous process of evolution and this next step. Whereas previously evolution was blind and instinctive, and hence from our stand-point of time immensely slow and delayed, now for the first time it is possible for human beings consciously to participate in and thus hasten the process of evolution. Sri Aurobindo has written volumes about this process of evolution, the difficulties and adverse forces that have to be overcome and the methods whereby they can be tackled. In his writings he has made an extraordinarily detailed and profound study of the various phases of human consciousness, and has also indicated the nature of the higher supra-mental plane. It is not necessary or possible here even to summarize what he has said. It must suffice to say that he evolved his own technique—which he termed Integral or *Purna* Yoga, incorporating elements of *Karma, Bhakti, Jnana* and *Raja Yogas*[1] as well as *Tantric*[2] principles—as the means whereby man could actively contribute towards a hastening of the evolutionary process. The key to his approach was for the Yogi to rise to the Supra-mental plane where the light and power of the Supermind constantly blazed forth, to incorporate that light in his consciousness, and then to descend back to the material plane so that the power of the Supra-mental itself could be brought to bear directly on this

[1] The four broad paths of Yoga (or 'Union' with the Supreme) outlined in Hinduism—the paths of desire-less action, emotional worship, intellectual discrimination and psycho-spiritual disciplines respectively.

[2] Esoteric worship of the great primal creatrix, symbolized by the female form of a goddess.

earth and thus hasten the evolutionary process.

This brings us to two unique features of Sri Aurobindo's Yoga. Firstly, he is emphatic that his Yoga is not merely directed towards individual salvation but is for humanity as a whole. Whereas traditional religions offered the devotee individual liberation from the bondage of material existence and a rise into the luminous spiritual sphere, Sri Aurobindo insisted that the ascent was only one aspect of the whole spiritual adventure. Having ascended the Yogi must again come down so that he can help the mass of humanity, and indeed all matter in whatsoever form, to rise.[1] Thus conceived, his *Weltanschauung* is stunning in its daring ambition and immensity. He sought not mere individual liberation, not liberation for the entire human race, not even liberation for all living beings, but nothing less than a complete transformation of material consciousness itself, the creation of 'a new heaven and a new earth'. The second feature of Sri Aurobindo's thought is that it attempts a final reconciliation between Spirit and Matter, a duality which has dogged philosophical speculation since its very inception. Matter is not different from Spirit, it is in fact only at a different level of evolution. Ultimately it will evolve into pure Spirit, that is, into its original state. Matter is spirit which is gross. Spirit is matter which is subtle. Both are aspects of the 'One Omnipresent Reality'.

Sri Aurobindo did not believe that there would be a sudden miraculous transformation of the human race *en masse* into a race of Supermen. He held that it was a slow and painful process, and that at first only a few of the more developed souls would emerge as pathfinders to point the way for the rest of humanity. As in the case of any new venture, these great souls would have to struggle and labour hard to hew out a track for others to follow. Often they would be overwhelmed by hostile forces and fall by the wayside. But sooner or later the path would be found, the trail blazed, and humanity will begin the next stage of its long, adventurous spiritual journey.

India has always had a deep and abiding tradition of spiritual thought and practice. It was thus only to be expected that in this great evolutionary leap forward India would take the lead.

[1] It must be remarked that this view has affinity with the Mahayana of Bodhisattvas and the traditional Hindu doctrine of Siddhas. Nevertheless, it has seldom been so clearly put forward as the spiritual goal as in the theory of Sri Aurobindo.

In fact, as will be clear from the survey of his concept of 'nation' and 'nationalism' that follows, Sri Aurobindo desired India to be politically free not only for her own sake but specifically because thereby alone could she play her true role in the spiritual regeneration of the world and in spearheading mankind's spiritual evolution. His Idealism, thus, is the firm foundation upon which he raises the imposing superstructure of his political theory.

7

HIS CONCEPT OF 'NATION'

'ALL great movements of life in India have begun with a new spiritual thought and usually a new religious activity.'[1] We have studied earlier how the renaissance in India and the gradual emergence in the nineteenth century of modern Indian nationalism were, in fact, determined largely by the religious and social reform movements resulting from the Western impact on the ancient Hindu culture of India. If Sri Aurobindo's aphorism is to be specifically applied, we might refer it to the publication in 1883 of the celebrated novel *Ananda Math* by the great Bengali novelist Bankim Chandra Chatterjee. It was this book that, as Sri Aurobindo puts it, 'gave us the reviving *mantra*[2] which is creating a new India, the mantra "Bande Mataram".'[3]

It is in this mantra 'Bande Mataram' (Hail to the Mother) that the key to the understanding of Sri Aurobindo's concept of the nation is to be found. For him India was no mere geographical entity, no mere physical and material land mass, no mere intellectual concept, but a Goddess incarnate, a mighty Mother who for centuries has cradled and nourished her children and who, at that time, was groaning under the yoke of the foreign oppressor—her pride shattered, her glory ground to the dust. In his famous 'Bhawani Mandir' scheme, which incidentally reveals the deep influence of Bankim's *Anand Math* not only in its underlying theory but even in its concrete proposal for a secret monastery where dedicated freedom fighters were to be trained for the liberation of the motherland, Sri Aurobindo writes: 'For what is a nation? What is our mother country? It is not a piece of earth, nor a figure of speech, nor a

---

[1] *The Renaissance in India* (Sri Aurobindo), p. 44.
[2] Mystic syllable or syllables, the repetition of which produces powerful spiritual effects.
[3] *Bande Mataram*, April 16, 1907.

fiction of the mind. It is a mighty *Shakti*,[1] composed of all the *Shakties* of all the millions of units that make up the nation, just as *Bhawāni Mahisha Mardini* sprang into being from the *Shakti* of all the millions of gods assembled in one mass of force and welded into unity.[2] The *Shakti* we call in India, *Bhawāni Bhārati*, is the living unity of the *Shakties* of three hundred million people. . . .'[3] In his essay on Bankim he says: 'It is not till the motherland reveals herself to the eye of the mind as something more than a sketch of earth or a mass of individuals, it is not till she takes shape as a great Divine and Maternal Power in a form of beauty that can dominate the mind and seize the heart, that these petty fears and hopes vanish in the all-absorbing passion for the Mother and her service, and the patriotism that works miracles and saves a doomed nation is born.'[4] The white heat of his spiritual patriotism is nowhere more clearly evident than in the following passage which is from an article intended for the Bande Mātaram but seized by the Police and used as an exhibit in the Alipore Conspiracy case:

'Love has a place in politics, but it is the love of one's country, for one's countrymen, for the glory, greatness and happiness of the race, the divine ananda of self-immolation for one's fellows, the ecstasy of relieving their sufferings, the joy of seeing one's blood flow for country and freedom, the bliss of union in death with the fathers of the race. The feeling of almost physical delight in the touch of the mother-soil, of the winds that blow from Indian seas, of the rivers that stream from Indian hills, in the hearing of Indian speech, music, poetry, in the familiar sights, sounds, habits, dress, manners of our Indian life, this is the physical root of that love. The pride in our past, the pain of our present, the passion for the future are its trunk and branches. Self-sacrifice and self-forgetfulness, great service, high endurance for the country are its fruit. And the sap which keeps it alive is the realization of the Motherhood of God in the

---

[1] Power.
[2] This refers to the incident related in the *Durga Saptshati* of the *Devi Bhagavatam*, when all the gods assemble and pool their powers resulting in the creation of the mighty Goddess *Bhāwani* who proceeds to slay the great oppressor demon *Mahishāsura* and free the land of his tyranny.
[3] 'Bhawāni Mandir' published in *Sri Aurobindo Mandir Annual*, Jayanti Number 15, August 15, 1956.
[4] *Bande Mataram*, April 16, 1907.

country, the vision of the Mother, the perpetual contemplation, adoration and service of the Mother."[1]

Such quotations from Sri Aurobindo's writings can be multi-plied, but from these extracts alone it is clear that his love for India and his concept of India as a nation was far deeper than the normal patriotism that everyone is expected to feel for one's country. He looked upon India as a living and pulsating spiritual entity. Thus in his beautiful verse translation of the song 'Bande Mātaram', which appeared in its original Sanskrit in Bankim's novel Ānand Math and which today is one of the two national songs of free India, he writes with lyrical beauty of his conception of Mother India:

> 'Mother I bow to thee!
> Rich with thy hurrying streams,
> Bright with thy orchard gleams,
> Cool with thy winds of delight,
> Dark fields waving, Mother of might,
> Mother free. . . .
>
> To thee I call, Mother and Lord!
> Thou who savest, arise and save!
> To her I cry who ever her foemen drave
> Back from plain and sea
> And shook herself free.
> Thou art wisdom, thou art law,
> Thou our heart, our soul, our breath,
> Thou the love divine, the awe
> In our hearts that conquers death.
> Thine the strength that nerves the arm,
> Thine the beauty, thine the charm.
> Every image made divine
> In our temples is but thine. . . .'[2]

This conception of the 'nation' is important for a correct under-standing of Sri Aurobindo's political thought, and from it his concept of 'Nationalism' flows logically.

[1] The Doctrine of Passive Resistance (Sri Aurobindo), pp. 83-84.

[2] Reproduced in Bankim—Tilak—Dayananda (Sri Aurobindo), pp. 3 and 4.

8

HIS CONCEPT OF 'NATIONALISM'

INDIA was indeed the Mother, but a mother in chains, a mother enslaved and humiliated by alien aggressors, a mother oppressed and starved by her foreign rulers. What is the duty of sons who find their mother, their goddess, reduced to this pitiable plight? If we accept Sri Aurobindo's premise, there is only one answer that he could and did give: they must strive by every possible means to liberate her from her shackles. In this task there can be no compromise, there is no question of bartering or bargaining with the Mother's liberty. Full and complete emancipation can be the only demand. And in the struggle the children must be prepared willingly to sacrifice everything in the service of the Mother, for is it not from Her that everything they have is derived? 'The work of national emancipation,' writes Sri Aurobindo, 'is a great and holy yajna[1] of which Boycott, Swadeshi, National Education and every other activity, great and small, are only major or minor parts. Liberty is the fruit we seek from the sacrifice and the Motherland the goddess to whom we offer it; into the seven leaping tongues of the fire of the yajna we must offer all that we are and all that we have, feeding the fire even with our blood and lives and happiness of our nearest and dearest; for the Motherland is a goddess who loves not a maimed and imperfect sacrifice, and freedom was never won from the gods by a grudging giver.'[2] In the same strain he writes: 'If any reservation mars the completeness of our self-abandonment, if any bargaining abridges the fullness of the sacrifice, if any doubt mars the strength of our faith and enthusiasm, if any thought of self pollutes the sanctity of our love, then the Mother will not be satisfied and will continue to withhold her presence.'[1]

[1] Sacrifice.
[2] *The Doctrine of Passive Resistance* (Sri Aurobindo), pp. 77-78. The Tantric aspect of Devi worship is clearly evident.

Nationalism in Sri Aurobindo's thought is thus not merely a patriotic and intellectual pastime but a deep and fervent religious *sadhana*.[2] In one of his speeches this is very clearly expressed 'What is Nationalism? Nationalism is not a mere political programme; nationalism is a religion that has come from God; Nationalism is a creed which you shall have to live. . . . If you are going to be a nationalist, if you are going to assent to this religion of nationalism, you must do it in the religious spirit. You must remember that you are the instruments of God.'[3]

Here we find the spiritual approach to politics, which was just emerging during the early Baroda period, in full bloom. And it is no mere rabble-rousing, demagogic trick. It is a conviction passionately held and eloquently expressed, and represents one of the keys to a correct interpretation of Sri Aurobindo's political thought, which may well be defined as 'spiritual nationalism'. In fact for a proper appraisal of this phase of Indian history we must grasp clearly this spiritual factor and this religious appeal, by means of which almost overnight the nationalist movement was converted from an intellectual pastime of the English-educated elite into a mass movement that created in the minds and hearts of the Indian people the will to freedom and the determination to achieve it at any cost. In Sri Aurobindo's thought the firm belief that India had a mighty role to play in the spiritual regeneration of the human race, and a divine mission to fulfil on earth, further strengthened his conviction that nothing less than absolute freedom, *Purna Swaraj*, could be the goal of genuine Indian nationalism. He sums this up when he writes in the *Bande Mātaram*:

'We recognize no political object of worship except the divinity in our Motherland, no present object of political endeavour except liberty, and no method or action as politically good or evil except as it truly helps or hinders our progress towards national emancipation.'[4]

And his flaming patriotism and religious devotion to Mother

---

[1] *Bande Mātaram* weekly ed., April 12, 1908.
[2] Discipline, practised for the attainment of a spiritual goal.
[3] *Speeches* (Sri Aurobindo), p. 6.
[4] *The Doctrine of Passive Resistance* (Sri. Aurobindo), pp. 67-68.

India is well reflected in his Speeches, such as when he exhorts the students of the Bengal National College in these terms:

'There are times in a nation's history when Providence places before it one work, one aim, to which everything else, however high and noble in itself, has to be sacrificed. Such a time has now arrived for our Motherland when nothing is dearer than her service, when everything else is to be directed to that end. If you will study, study for her sake; train yourselves body and mind and soul for her service. You will earn your living that you may live for her sake. You will go abroad to foreign lands that you may bring back knowledge with which you may do service to her. Work that she may prosper. Suffer that she may rejoice. All is contained in that one single advice.'[1]

As a natural concomitant of his theory of spiritual nationalism we find that Sri Aurobindo frequently and unabashedly claims that the nationalist movement sparked off by the Bengal partition was a divinely inspired and divinely guided movement. This is particularly evident in the inspiring and eloquent speeches he delivered during the fateful days of the anti-partition agitation. Speaking of its leaders he says:

'They have had one and all of them, consciously or unconsciously, one overmastering idea, one idea which nothing can shake, and this was the idea that there is a great Power at work to help India, and that we are doing what it bids us. . . . This movement in Bengal, this movement of nationalism is not guided by any self-interest, not at the heart of it. Whatever there may be in some minds, it is not, at the heart of it, a political self-interest that we are pursuing. It is a religion which we are trying to live. It is a religion by which we are trying to realize God in the nation, in our fellow-countrymen.'[2]

In another speech he says:

'Nationalism is a religion that has come from God. . . . It has not been crushed. It is not going to be crushed. Nationalism survives in the strength of God and it is not possible to crush it, whatever weapons are brought against it. Nationalism is im-

---

[1] *Speeches* (Sri Aurobindo), p. 4.
[2] *Ibid*, pp. 18-19.

mortal, Nationalism cannot die, because it is no human thing, it is God who is working in Bengal.'[1]

Similarly, in one of his inspiring editorials in the *Bande Mātaram*, he writes:

'The bureaucracy will not have to reckon this time with a few self-styled leaders who are only too eager to fall down and worship the idol of the hour, but with a newly-awakened people to whom the political freedom of the country has been elevated to the height of a religious faith. . . . The political strife has assumed a religious character, and the question now before the people is whether India—the India of the holy Rishis, the India that gave birth to a Rama, a Krishna and a Buddha, the India of Sivaji and Guru Gobinda—is destined for ever to lie prostrate at the proud feet of a conqueror. Are we going to sacrifice our national destiny to the whims and interests of the foreigner or are we again to take ourselves seriously and struggle for the right to live that we may fulfil in this world our Heaven-appointed mission?'[2]

Nationalism was thus considered by Sri Aurobindo to be a much deeper and more profound concept than mere patriotism. In consonance with his concept of the nation as a divine entity, he looked upon nationalism as a spiritual imperative, a virtually religious practice which was essential for the emancipation of the motherland as well as the spiritual development of the devotee. This view was poles apart from the much less inspiring outlook of the Moderates who hankered after petty administrative and political reforms, and it is not difficult to see why this ideology swept all before it and brought about a mass awakening and revival in the Indian body politic. It must be added, however, that to his great credit Sri Aurobindo never allowed his nationalism to degenerate into mere chauvinism or narrow revivalism. In fact, as we have seen, he looked upon India's emancipation as only an essential vantage point from which she could fulfil her destiny as the spiritual guide of humanity at large. His nationalism thus develops logically into an internationalism that has as its goal the elevated ideal of human unity.

[1] Quoted by S. K. Mitra in *Sri Aurobindo and Indian Freedom*, p. 53.
[2] *Bande Mātaram* weekly ed., December 1, 1907.

Even at the risk of digressing somewhat from our main theme, it is necessary here to deal briefly with a criticism that is sometimes levelled against the nationalism of Sri Aurobindo and other Radical leaders of his time, notably Tilak. It is said that the Radicals appealed to Hindu chauvinism to gain popularity, thus widening the rift between the Hindus and the Muslims which finally culminated in the partition of the country. A detailed analysis of this interesting problem is outside the scope of this work. Here it must suffice to point out that the key role of the Radicals was to transform the national movement from a narrow intellectual pastime of the English-educated intelligentsia into a broad mass movement. This transformation, in bringing about which they were successful despite severe British repression, could not have been achieved unless the masses—the vast majority of which were Hindus—were galvanized and awoken from their stupor. This in turn was impossible unless they were touched at their deepest level which, in a country like India with its age-old civilization based predominantly on Hinduism, could not have been any other than the religious. When we add to this the fact that most of the Radical leaders were Hindus of deep religious and spiritual convictions, it is clear that their appeal to the masses could not have been couched in non-religious terms. Thus, without any intention to under-rate, far less attack, any of the other great religions of India, the Radical philosophy necessarily appealed primarily to the Hindus.

It is, however, interesting and important to point out that Sri Aurobindo was quite clear about the importance of evoking Muslim support in the great cause of nationalism. Thus at the very height of the partition agitation he wrote: 'Nationalism depends for its success on the awakening and organizing of the whole strength of the nation, it is therefore vitally important for nationalism that the politically backward classes should be awakened and brought into the current of political life; the great mass of orthodox Hinduism which was hardly ever touched by the old Congress movement the great slumbering mass of Islam which has remained politically inert throughout the last century, the shopkeepers, the artisan class, the immense body of illiterate and ignorant peasantry, the submerged classes, even the wild tribes and races still outside the pale of Hindu civilization, Nationalism can afford to neglect and omit none.

It rejoices to see any sign of life where there was no life before, even if its first manifestations should seem to be ill-regulated or misguided. It is not afraid of Pan-Islamism or any signs of the growth of a separate Mohammedan self-consciousness but rather welcomes them."[1]

[1] *Bande Mātaram*, 22.12.1907. Article on 'The Awakening of Gujarat'.

9

HIS POLITICAL GOAL

SRI AUROBINDO'S political goal for India was nothing less than complete freedom from foreign domination. He poured scorn and contempt upon the limited demands of the Moderates for expansion of the Legislative bodies, progressive Indianization of the Indian Civil Service, tariff protection for Indian industries and so on. In his view these minor administrative and economic reforms were utterly worthless without national freedom.

The question can now be posed as to why Sri Aurobindo desired nothing less than absolute freedom for his country, at a time when the idea appeared utterly impractical and impossible of achievement.[1] From a study of his writings, the answer to this lies broadly in two directions. Firstly, in accordance with his idealistic and spiritual approach which we have surveyed, he looked upon the motherland as a Divine Mother for whose emancipation her children must strive with all their power. It was not only for her own sake, however, that India must be free, but for all Humanity. This will become clear by a reference to his theory of spiritual evolution. He firmly held the view that it is India that is destined to spearhead the next phase of human evolution, because it is her *Swadharma*, or essential nature, to guide the world on the spiritual path. But she cannot rise to her full spiritual stature and show the way to the rest of the world as long as she is fettered and shackled by foreign rulers who, though materially powerful, are spiritually very far behind her. How can she fulfil her predestined spiritual role as the 'guru of nations' as long as she is bound hand and foot, her great spirit confined and constricted. Therefore the first pre-requisite is for India to become free, so that she can fulfil her

[1] *Cf.* the celebrated statement by the great Moderate leader, G. K. Gokhale, 'Only men outside lunatic asylums could think or talk of independence . . . there is no alternative to British rule, not only now but for a long time to come . . .' (*Speeches*, p. 1148.)

Swadharma and spread the spiritual message throughout the world. In *Bhawāni Mandir* Sri Aurobindo states this concept very clearly and unequivocally. He says:

'India must be Reborn, because her Rebirth is demanded by the future of the world: India cannot perish, our race cannot become extinct, because among all the divisions of mankind it is to India that is reserved the highest and the most splendid destiny, the most essential to the future of the human race. It is she who must send forth from herself the future religion of the entire world, the Eternal religion which is to harmonize all religion, science and philosophies and make mankind one soul.'

In his famous Uttarapura speech Sri Aurobindo declared:

'This is the *Dharma* that for the salvation of humanity was cherished in the seclusion of this peninsula from of old. It is to give this religion that India is rising. She does not rise as other countries do, for self or when she is strong, to trample on the weak. She is rising to shed the eternal light entrusted to her over the world. India has always existed for humanity and not for herself and it is for humanity and not for herself that she must be great.'[1]

And later in the same speech, when he mentions his prayers for guidance while in Alipore jail, he says he received this divine reply: 'I am raising up this nation to send forth my word.' As an even more explicit statement of Sri Aurobindo's doctrine that India must be free so that she can fulfil her divinely appointed spiritual mission, we may quote the following lines from an Editorial written by him in the *Bande Mātaram* weekly edition of May 3, 1908:

'The ideal of unqualified *Swaraj* has a charm for the national mind which is irresistible if it is put before it in the national way by minds imbued with Indian feeling and free from the gross taint of Western materialism. *Swaraj* as a sort of European ideal, political liberty for the sake of political self-assertion, will not awaken India. *Swaraj* as the fulfilment of the ancient life of India under modern conditions, the return of the *Satyayuga*[1] of

---

[1] *Speeches* (Sri Aurobindo), p. 63.

national greatness, the resumption by her of her great role of teacher and guide, self-liberation of the people for the final fulfilment of the *Vedantic* ideal in politics, this is the true *Swaraj* for India. Of all the proud nations of the West there is an end determined. When their limited special work for mankind is done they must decay and disappear. But the function of India is to supply the world with a perennial source of light and renovation. Whenever the first play of energy is exhausted and earth grows old and weary, full of materialism, racked with problems she cannot solve, the function of India is to restore the youth of mankind and assure it of immortality. She sends forth a light from her bosom which floods the earth and the heavens, and mankind bathes in it like St George in the well of life and recovers strength, hope and vitality for its long pilgrimage. Such a time is now at hand. The world needs India and needs her free. The work she has to do now is to organize life in the terms of *Vedanta*, and that is a work she cannot do while overshadowed by a foreign power and a foreign civilization. She cannot do it without taking the management of her own life into her own hands. She must live her own life and not the life of a part or subordinate in a foreign Empire.'

We see, therefore, that freedom was for Sri Aurobindo no mere political goal, no mere realignment of constitutional provisions, but a deep and fundamental spiritual necessity without which India as a nation would perish and humanity would lose for ever the spiritual light that she could, if she were free from alien bonds, spread throughout the world. It is in this strain that he writes:

'It is idle to believe that we can even think of regaining our spiritual greatness without re-establishing our normal political relation with the other advanced peoples of the world. In fact the true aim of the nationalist movement is to restore the spiritual greatness of the nation by the essential preliminary of its political generation.'[2]

'*Swaraj*,' he says in one of his speeches, 'is not the colonial form of Government nor any form of Government. It means the fulfilment of our national life. That is what we seek, that is

---

[1] The golden age.
[2] *Bande Mataram*, 10. 11. 1907.

F

why God has sent us into the world to fulfil him by fulfilling ourselves in our individual life, in the family, in the community, in the nation, in humanity. That is why he has sent us to the world and it is this fulfilment that we demand, for this fulfilment is life and to depart from it is to perish. Our object, our claim is that we shall not perish as a nation, but live as a nation."[1]

Apart from his spiritual idealism and his desire to see India play her destined role in the spiritual regeneration of the world, however, Sri Aurobindo had another more secular reason for taking complete freedom as his political goal. This was his conviction that no real development was possible in India—be it economic, social, administrative or any other—unless she was first free of her foreign rulers. In other words, political freedom was the *sine qua non* of all other progress in India, hence his stress on the primacy of political emancipation over such matters as social, economic and administrative reform which were the main planks of the Moderate platform. Writing in the *Bande Mātaram*[2] he clearly expressed this view when he wrote:

'No national self-development is possible without the support of *Rajashakti*, organized political strength, commanding and wherever necessary compelling general allegiance and obedience. . . . Political freedom is the life-breath of a nation; to attempt social reform, educational reform, industrial expansion, the moral improvement of the race without aiming first and foremost at political freedom, is the very height of ignorance and futility. Such attempts are predoomed to disappointment and failure; yet when the disappointment and failure come we choose to attribute them to some radical defect in the national character; as if the nation were at fault and not its wise men who would not or could not understand the first elementary conditions of success. The primary requisite for national progress, national reform, is the free habit of free and healthy national thought and action which is impossible in a state of servitude. The second is the organization of the national will in a strong central authority.'

Sri Aurobindo clearly saw that a century and a half of British rule had brought India to the verge of complete ruin, both moral and material. He wrote:

[1] *Speeches* (Sri Aurobindo), pp. 85-86.
[2] April 9, 1907.

'Morally and materially she has been brought to the verge of exhaustion and decay by the bureaucratic rule and any further acquiescence in servitude will result in that death-sleep of centuries from which a nation, if it ever awakes at all, awakes emaciated, feeble and unable to resume its true rank in the list of the peoples.'[1]

Thus India could not afford to hanker after petty reforms on which, as he caustically remarked, the Moderates had 'mis-spent half a century of unavailing effort'; reforms that would leave the basic structure of subservience to a foreign power and an alien culture untouched. The immediate problem was how to arrest the decay that had set in in the body politic of India or, as he put it, 'how to stave off imminent national death, how to put an end to the white peril, how to assert ourselves and live.'[2] All energies must therefore be turned towards the achievement of national freedom, and not frittered away in the pursuit of less exalted goals which would leave the fundamental problem untouched.

This view was held very strongly by Sri Aurobindo and explains the scorn and ridicule he poured upon the Moderates and their moderate demands which, in the light of prevailing conditions, appeared to him to be little short of treason to the nation. He says in one of his speeches[3]:

'Our ideal is that of *Swaraj* or absolute autonomy free from foreign control. We claim the right of every nation to live its own life by its own energies according to its own nature and ideals. We reject the claim of aliens to force upon us a civilization inferior to our own or to keep us out of our inheritance on the untenable ground of a superior fitness. While admitting the stains and defects which long subjection has induced upon our native capacity and energy, we are conscious of that capacity and energy reviving in us. . . . All we need is a field and an opportunity. That field and opportunity can only be provided by a national government, and free society and a great Indian culture. So long as these are not conceded to us, we can have no other use for our brains, courage and capacity than to struggle unceasingly to achieve them.'

[1] *The Doctrine of Passive Resistance* (Sri Aurobindo), p. 33.
[2] *Ibid*, p. 26.
[3] *Speeches* (Sri Aurobindo), pp. 140-41.

83

One of the great achievements of the Nationalist party, and of its eloquent organ the *Bande Mātaram* edited by Sri Aurobindo, was to bring for the first time before the Indian public the invigorating ideal of complete *Swaraj*. While the venerable Moderate leadership continued to press for this or that minor reform, the Nationalists went to the heart of the matter and thus won the heart of the masses. Under Sri Aurobindo's fearless advocacy the question of partition of Bengal receded into the background and, as Professor P. C. Chakravarti puts it:

'The issue which was openly raised was not whether Bengal should be one unpartitioned province or two partitioned provinces under British rule, but whether British rule was to endure in Bengal or, for the matter of that, anywhere in India.[1]

Thus the political genius of Sri Aurobindo seized upon the crisis caused by Curzon's partition of Bengal to bring before his countrymen the clear, unambiguous, unequivocal and inspiring ideal of complete freedom from foreign rule. In the course of a speech in 1909[2] he said:

'We preach the gospel of unqualified *Swaraj*. There are some who fear to use the word "freedom", but I have always used the word because it has been the *mantra* of my life to aspire towards the freedom of my country.'

Looked at in historical perspective it is clear that the work of the nationalists in bringing to the forefront the doctrine of *Purna Swaraj* rendered incalculable service to the cause of India's freedom. At the time, however, they came under heavy fire— not only from the British, which was only to be expected—but from the Moderates who charged them with ignoring other more urgent issues and advocating instead an utterly unreal and impractical creed. To this charge Sri Aurobindo's reply was clear and unfaltering. He wrote:

'The Nationalist has been putting the main stress on the necessity of political freedom almost to the exclusion of the other needs of the nation, not because he is not alive to the vital im-

[1] Article on 'Sri Aurobindo and the Indian Freedom Movement' published in *Loving Homage*, pp. 270-297.
[2] Delivered at Jhalakati in Barisal, June, 1909.

portance of those needs of economic renovation, of education, of social transformation, but because he knows that in order that his ideal of equality may be brought to its fullest fruition, he must first bring about the political freedom and federation of his country."[1]

Future events showed how unerringly Sri Aurobindo had grasped the true essence of the political problem in India, for while the Moderates were swept into the backwaters of history the Radical creed swept irresistibly forward to a triumphant conclusion in his very lifetime.

[1] *Bande Mātaram*, weekly edition, September 22, 1907.

PART IV

SRI AUROBINDO AS A RADICAL LEADER —HIS TECHNIQUE OF POLITICAL ACTION

10

SRI AUROBINDO'S APPROACH TO POLITICAL TECHNIQUE

'THE ideal creates the means of attaining the ideal, if it is itself true and rooted in the destiny of the race.'[1]

The previous chapter reviewed the philosophical background of Sri Aurobindo's political thought, founded as it is on the Idealistic basis of his 'spiritual nationalism'. This inevitably led to his adopting as the goal of his political endeavours nothing less than the complete emancipation of his motherland from foreign rule. If his masterly theoretical exposition of this ideal and this goal had been Sri Aurobindo's only contribution, this alone would have entitled him to an honoured place among modern Indian political thinkers. But Sri Aurobindo did more than this. He sought to draw up a concrete programme of political action whereby the goal could be achieved, and to this end he wrote and spoke profusely regarding the technique of practical politics. He was thus one of those rare figures in political history—a profound theoretician who was at the same time a clever and discerning political tactician.

In this Part we will attempt to study the technique of political action which Sri Aurobindo advocated. As this has many facets it will be convenient to discuss it under various headings, but it must be kept in mind that in politics as in the spiritual quest Sri Aurobindo's approach was integral and syncretic, and though we may try and isolate the various factors in his approach these in fact form inter-twining strands of a coherent and integrated approach to the political problem.

Before studying in detail Sri Aurobindo's political technique, it is of interest to note the type of methods that he disapproved of and severely attacked. These were the 'mendicant' methods adopted by the Moderates in their relations with the British,

---

[1] *Bande Mātaram*, weekly edition, May 3, 1908.

which he contemptuously dismissed as a bankrupt policy of 'prayer, petition and protest'. The political goal that the Moderates set before themselves was in fact much less inspiring and bold than that of the Extremists. It consisted in the widening of popular representation in the legislatures, increasing Indianization of the Indian Civil Service and the Indian Army Officers Corps, the protection of Indian industries from foreign competition by the erection of tariff walls, the increasing responsiveness of British administrators to the needs of their Indian subjects and numerous other matters of like nature, all very laudable and desirable but—when compared to the Extremist credo of complete independence—strictly limited in scope. For the attainment of these ends it was but logical that the Moderates should bank on the enlightened support of the British, and refrain from any action or speech that might unduly ruffle their tempers. Thus we find the Congress resolutions before the rise of the Extremist party full of praises for the British and of laudatory remarks regarding the advantages that had accrued to India from their rule. Interspersed with such sentiments were very moderate political demands, often put forward in a hesitant and almost apologetic manner.[1] It was this that infuriated Sri Aurobindo. He condemned in no uncertain terms this approach whereby the initiative was always in the hands of the British Government. For tactical reasons the foreign rulers would from time to time fling a few crumbs of concession

---

[1] For example, even as late as 1908, after the Radicals had broken away the previous year at Surat, the Moderate-dominated Congress passed such servile resolutions as the following: 'The Indian National Congress tenders its loyal homage to His Gracious Majesty the King Emperor and respectfully welcomes the message sent by His Majesty to the Princes and People of India on the Fiftieth Anniversary of the Memorable Proclamation issued in 1858 by his Illustrious Mother VICTORIA THE GOOD. This Congress begs to record its satisfaction that the interpretation placed by it upon the pledges contained in that "Great Charter of 1858" has been upheld by His Majesty.

This Congress gratefully welcomes the pronouncement made by His Majesty that the time has come when the principle of representative institutions, which, from the first, began to be gradually introduced in India, may be prudently extended and that the politic satisfaction of the claim to equality of citizenship and greater share in legislation and Government made by important classes in India, representing ideas that have been fostered and encouraged by British rule, will strengthen, not impair, existing authority and power.'

(Resolution No. 1 of the 23rd Indian National Congress held at Madras on 28th, 29th and 30th December, 1908.)

and minor reform from their table, which the Moderates would pounce upon with joyful expressions of pleasure and gratitude.

From the analysis of Sri Aurobindo's first political writings in the *Indu Prakash*, it is evident that right from the beginning he grasped clearly that if India was to achieve anything from her alien rulers she must do so by dint of her own struggle and sacrifice, by an appeal to her own immense potential of power rather than the condescension of her rulers. Thus he also rejected the policy, advocated among others by his friend and colleague Bipin Chandra Pal, of Indian leaders going to England and seeking to convert British public opinion there in the mistaken view that the British could be persuaded by mere words into giving up their political and economic interests in India. He dismissed 'the fable that speeches and Congress in England can change an ignorant British public into informed and enthusiastic supporters of Indian self-government' and added that 'it is only political necessity and the practical recognition that change is inevitable which can convert the statesmen of England.'[1]

As we saw in a previous chapter on the goal of Sri Aurobindo's political endeavours, for him there was 'only one political question and one aim, not the gradual improvement of the present administration into something in the end fundamentally the opposite of itself, but the early substitution of Indian and national for English and bureaucratic control in the affairs of India.'[2] He adds 'A subject nation does not prepare itself by gradual progress for liberty; it opens by liberty its way to rapid progress.'[3]

---

[1] The *Karmayogin*, August 28, 1959, article entitled 'London Congress'. Also see *Karmayogin*, October 9, 1909, on 'Nationalist work in England'.

[2] Introduction to 'Speeches and writings of Tilak', 1918. Printed in *Bankim-Tilak-Dayananda*.

[3] This was of course diametrically opposed to the Moderate doctrine of gradualism. A classic statement of this doctrine, liberally garnished with naïve wishful thinking, is to be found in Rash Behari Ghosh's undelivered Presidential Address for the 1907 session of the Congress which broke up in confusion at Surat. Therein the Moderate leader, addressing the members of the new Radical party, said: 'I implore you not to persevere in your present course. Do not be beguiled by mere phantoms. You cannot put an end to British rule by boycotting the administration. Your only chance under the present circumstances of gaining your object lies in co-operation with the Government in every measure which is likely to hasten our political emancipation; for so long as we do not show ourselves worthy of it, rely upon it England will maintain her rule, and if you really want self-government you

A detailed review of the various methods which Sri Aurobindo advocated for the attainment of this liberty for his motherland can conveniently be made under the following heads, each dealing with one distinct facet of his political technique:

The revival of the national spirit and pride in India's great cultural heritage;

Direct revolutionary action: Terrorism and armed revolt; Passive resistance and boycott. This last can further be subdivided into:

(a) Economic boycott and *swadeshi*,
(b) Educational boycott and national education,
(c) Judicial boycott and national arbitration courts,
(d) Executive boycott and national organization,
(e) Social boycott.

must show that you are fit for such responsibility. Then and then only will the English retire from India, their task completely accomplished, and their duty done.'

11

REVIVAL OF INDIA'S NATIONAL SPIRIT

BEFORE Indian Independence could come within the realm of possibility, it was essential that large sections of the population should really come to desire this deeply and be prepared to make great sacrifices for it. It was also essential that they should feel that if a real effort was made there was a good chance of success. Now that it has been free for over a decade and a half we take it for granted that India is eminently fit for freedom, but at the turn of the century widespread apathy and despair pervaded the country and there were many who thought it was foolishly impractical even to talk of getting rid of British rule. The first and most fundamental battle, therefore, that Sri Aurobindo and his fellow nationalists had to fight was against this psychological barrier that existed in the minds of large sections of their countrymen. As he writes:

'We must first ourselves be free in heart before our country is free.'[1]

For this purpose the obvious procedure was to re-instil in the minds of Indians pride in the glorious cultural heritage that their forefathers had left them, an awareness of the great heights to which India had risen in the past, of her great achievements in the realm of politics and social organization, art and architecture, literature and learning and—above all—her unique contribution in the realm of religion and philosophy.

We have seen earlier in this work how the renaissance of Indian thought began in Bengal in the middle of the nineteenth century, and how great thinkers and leaders arose who re-introduced Indians to their distinguished past and laid before them prospects of a still more glorious future. Thus Raja Rammohan

[1] *Bande Mātaram*, weekly edition, April 12, 1908.

Roy, Bankim Chandra Chatterjee and others led the secular and literary revival, while the spiritual renaissance was generated by the great Ramakrishna Paramhansa and his remarkable group of disciples led by Swami Vivekananda, and also by Swami Dayananda Saraswati and the spiritual leaders of Maharashtra. This work of national revival and its spirituo-intellectual regeneration was carried a step further by the Nationalist leaders who, for the first time, succeeded in taking the message of hope and freedom to the masses. In an eloquent tribute to Bal Gangadhar Tilak, Sri Aurobindo well describes this achievement, to which his own contribution was substantial, in these words:

'The Congress movement was for a long time purely occidental in its mind, character and methods, confined to the English-educated few, founded on the political rights and interests of the people read in the light of English history and European ideals, but with no roots either in the past of the country or in the inner spirit of the nation. Mr Tilak was the first political leader to break through the routine of its somewhat academical methods, to bridge the gulf between the present and the past and to restore continuity to the political life of the nation. He developed a language and a spirit and he used methods which Indianized the movement and brought it into the masses.'[1]

Later in the same article he describes the crux of the nationalist creed when he says:

'To bring in the mass of the people, to found the greatness of the future on the greatness of the past, to infuse Indian politics with Indian religious fervour and spirituality are the indispensable conditions for a great and powerful political awakening in India.'

In his own writings Sri Aurobindo made a powerful contribution to this national awakening, though the fact that he wrote in English led to his greatest impact being on the minds of the English-educated intelligentsia.[2] Before 1910 his masterly

---

[1] Introduction to Speeches and Writings of Tilak, 1918. Printed in *Bankim-Tilak-Dayananda*.

[2] His outstanding role is well brought out in the following words by his

editorials, first in the *Bande Māharam* and then the *Karmayogin*, dealt with an astonishing array of subjects, all of which he illuminated with his deep knowledge of Indian culture. Whether it was the social organization of the early Aryans, the great achievements of Indian art, the current social, economic and political problems of the day—in everything he sought to bring home to his readers the genius and originality of Indian thought and the fact that in hardly any matter could the British surpass what Indian thinkers had already achieved. Thus, for example, in writing on 'The boycott celebration'[1] he analysed the importance of national festivals and pointed out that they are 'symbols of national vitality' and 'the first movements of a great national resurgence'. He referred approvingly to the Ganapati and Shivaji festivals launched by Tilak in Maharashtra, which had galvanized the people with a new pride in their heritage and a new vision of the future. Similarly he deprecated the distorted and one-sided view of Indian history that the British had caused to be placed before India and the world, and called for a fresh re-interpretation of Indian history to bring out the true glory and achievements of the race.[2]

It may be repeated here that Sri Aurobindo was no crude, narrow revivalist for whom everything indigenous was good

great contemporary Bipin Chandra Pal, which occur in his book *Indian Nationalism: Its Personalities and Principles*:

'The youngest in age among those who stand in the forefront of the Nationalist propaganda in India, but in endowment, education and Character, perhaps superior to them all—Aravinda seems distinctly marked out by Providence to play the future of this movement a part not given to any of his colleagues and contemporaries. . . . The Nationalist School was without a daily English organ. A new paper was started. Aravinda was invited to join its staff. A joint stock company was floated to run it, and Aravinda became one of the directors. This paper—*Bande Mātaram*—at once secured for itself a recognized position in Indian journalism. The hand of the master was in it from the very beginning. Its bold attitude, its vigorous thinking, its clear ideas, its chaste and powerful diction, its scorching sarcasm and refined witticism were unsurpassed by any journal in the country, either Indian or Anglo-Indian. It at once raised the tone of every Bengalee paper, and compelled the admiration of even hostile Anglo-Indian editors. Morning after morning not only Calcutta, but the educated community almost in every part of the country eagerly awaited its vigorous pronouncements on the stirring questions of the day. . . . It was a force in the country which none dared to ignore, however much they might fear or hate it, and Aravinda was the leading spirit, the central figure, in the new journal.'

[1] *Karmayogin*, August 14, 1909.

[2] See 'Suprabhat', *Karmayogin*, August 14, 1909.

and everything foreign bad. On the contrary he had a clear awareness of the depths to which his country had fallen and the shortcomings of its national spirit and life. He felt strongly, however, that these misfortunes were not the result of any ingrained weakness in the Indian character—as the British often sought to prove—but were due merely to a temporary set of unfavourable circumstances, the most adverse of which was the very fact of alien rule. He felt that a revival and regeneration of true Indian culture was a pre-requisite for her political freedom, and all his political writings were directed towards encouraging and hastening such a revival. As spiritualism was the keynote of Sri Aurobindo's approach to political thought and action, the regeneration that he aspired towards was no mere growth of national chauvinism but a deep spiritual rebirth. He writes:

'Those who have freed nations have first passed through the agony of utter renunciation before their efforts were crowned with success, and those who aspire to free India will first have to pay the price which the Mother demands. . . . Regeneration is literally rebirth, and rebirth comes not by the intellect, not by the fullness of the purse, not by policy, not by change of machinery, but by getting a new heart, by throwing away all into the fire of sacrifice and being reborn in the Mother.'[1]

After his departure for Pondicherry in 1910 there was a period of about four years in which Sri Aurobindo did not write very much. Then, on August 15, 1914, he began the publication of a journal called the *Ārya* to which he contributed profusely for many years. It was through the medium of this publication that he poured out his views on an incredibly diverse spectrum of topics, on all of which he brought to bear his vast erudition and his integral vision of life. Running throughout these remarkable writings is the same trend that was evident before 1910, the revival of India's great cultural heritage, the re-appreciation of her outstanding achievements in almost all spheres of human thought and activity, and the re-statement of the true values in Indian culture that had been—out of ignorance or sheer malice—grossly misinterpreted by Western commentators. Thus from December 15, 1918 to January 15, 1921, he published a series of articles which have been col-

[1] *Bande Mātaram*, weekly edition, April 12, 1908.

lectively printed under the title *Foundations of Indian Culture*. This work is a remarkable analysis of the bases upon which Indian civilization was built and survived all vicissitudes down through the centuries, and it effectively refutes the shallow, ignorant and often deliberately malicious criticisms that were in those days frequently levied against Indian art and culture by Western litterateurs. In fact the essays were undertaken as a reply to a considerable work by one Mr William Archer entitled *Is India civilized* in which he criticized and attacked Indian civilization and culture in all its domains. Sri Aurobindo's main object was to combat the self-depreciation awakened in the Indian mind by this hostile impact and to explain to it the true meaning of its own civilization and its great achievements. Thus he deprecates the 'low, imitative, un-Indian and bourgeois ideals of our national activity in the nineteenth century' and stresses 'the cardinal fact that, if India is to arise and be great as a nation, it is not by imitating the methods and institutions of English politics and commerce, but by carrying her own civilization, purified of the weaknesses that have overtaken it, to a much higher and mightier fulfilment than any it has reached in the past.'[1]

It is not possible here to enter into a detailed analysis of these and other writings of Sri Aurobindo on the wide panorama of Indian civilization. The point is to emphasize that for him the creation in the Indian mind of a proper appreciation of its civilization and culture, leading to the revival of her national spirit and pride in her heritage, was a definite technique whereby he hoped to create a favourable base for the success of the more direct political struggle. In this task he met with no inconsiderable success, working as he did upon the time-proven concept that the will-to-freedom was the first step towards its actual realization.

Another aspect of this approach is to be found in Sri Aurobindo's repeated exhortations to his people to be brave and to face suffering cheerfully for the sake of their motherland. Centuries of foreign rule had softened the Indian spirit, and people had been over-awed by the mighty power of the British Empire upon which the sun never set. Sri Aurobindo saw clearly that this timidity would be fatal to the success of the movement for national emancipation, and hence he laid great

[1] *Karmayogin*, 25.9.1909. Article on 'The past and the future'.

stress upon the necessity for sacrifice on the part of the Indian people if they were ever to gain their freedom. Writing in the *Bande Mātaram* he says:

'Plain speaking may be unpalatable and persecutions may follow, but persecutions have never yet killed a religious faith and a self-conscious India is too mighty a power to be put down by a despot's rod. Persecutions do not crush but only fortify conviction, and no power on earth can exterminate the seed of liberty when it has once germinated in the blood of earnest and sincere men.'[1]

The price of freedom in pain and suffering has to be paid, and Sri Aurobindo deprecated the view that in India freedom would be achieved without having to pay this price.[2] He writes: 'Politics is for the *Kshatriya*[3] and in the *Kshatriya* spirit alone can freedom and greatness be attained, not by the spirit of the *Baniya*[4] trying to buy freedom in the cheapest market and beat down the demands of Fate to a miser's niggard price. That which other nations have paid for freedom we also must pay, the path they have followed we also must follow.[5] He constantly stressed the need for India to shake off her centuries-old lethargy and become galvanized again with strength and power. In *Bhavāni Mandir* he writes:

'The deeper we look, the more we shall be convinced that the one thing wanting, which we must strive to acquire before all others, is strength—strength physical, strength mental, strength moral, but above all strength spiritual which is the one inexhaustible and imperishable source of all the others. If we have strength everything will be added to us easily and naturally. In the absence of strength we are like men in a dream who have hands but cannot seize or strike, who have feet but cannot run.'

[1] *Bande Mātaram*, weekly edition, December 1, 1907.

[2] It is interesting to note that although India did in 1947 achieve her independence 'peacefully', this is only true vis-à-vis the British. The appalling violence and suffering which occurred internally as the result of partition was certainly a substantial 'price' that had to be paid for freedom!

[3] The warrior class in the four-fold traditional Hindu caste structure.

[4] The merchant or trading class.

[5] *Bande Mātaram*, weekly edition, December 8, 1907. See also Karmayogin February 5, 1910—'Liberty is a goddess who is exacting her demands on her votaries, but if they are faithful she never disappoints them of their reward.'

The revival of a virile and powerful national spirit, and a climate of sacrifice and struggle, were thus an important feature of Sri Aurobindo's technique of political action.

12

DIRECT REVOLUTIONARY ACTION: TERRORISM AND ARMED REVOLT

'THE choice by a subject nation of the means it will use for vindicating its liberty,' writes Sri Aurobindo, 'is best determined by the circumstances of its servitude'. One of the courses . . . 'open to an oppressed nation is that of armed revolt. . . . This is the old time-honoured method which the oppressed or enslaved have always adopted by preference in the past and will adopt in the future if they see any chance of success; for it is the readiest and swiftest, the most thorough in its results, and demands the least powers of endurance and suffering and the smallest and briefest sacrifices.'[1] In this chapter we will seek to show that though Sri Aurobindo did advocate for his Nationalist party a policy of passive resistance, this was by no means based on any moral aversion to the use of force, but merely because, as he puts it, 'The present circumstances in India seem to point to passive resistance as our most natural and suitable weapon.'[2] In other words, passive resistance is advocated as a tactical manoeuvre, as the best policy to use at that particular juncture in the struggle against the British.[3]

Sri Aurobindo made no secret of his view that force and violence may be justified in the struggle for national emancipation. Nowhere has he stated this in clearer terms than in the article quoted above. Immediately after his statement regarding passive resistance he goes on to say:

'We would not for a moment be understood to base this conclusion upon any condemnation of other methods as in all

[1] *Doctrine of Passive Resistance*, pp. 28-29.
[2] *Ibid.*
[3] In this respect there is a sharp divergence between Sri Aurobindo's views and those of Mahatma Gandhi, who sought to raise *Ahimsa* or non-violence to the level of an eternal moral principle.

circumstances criminal and unjustifiable. It is the common habit of established Governments, and especially those which are themselves oppressors, to brand all violent methods in subject peoples and communities as criminal and wicked. . . . But no nation yet has listened to the cant of the oppressor when itself put to the test, and the general conscience of humanity approves the refusal. Under certain circumstances a civil struggle becomes in reality a battle and the morality of war is different from the morality of peace. To shrink from bloodshed and violence under such circumstances is a weakness deserving as severe a rebuke as Sri Krishna addressed to Arjuna when he shrank from the colossal civil slaughter on the field of Kurukshetra. Liberty is the life-breath of a nation; and when the life is attacked, when it is sought to suppress all chance of breathing by violent pressure, any and every means of self-preservation becomes right and justifiable—just as it is lawful for a man who is being strangled to rid himself of the pressure on his throat by any means in his power. It is the nature of the pressure which determines the nature of the resistance. Where, as in Russia, the denial of liberty is enforced by legalized murder and outrage, or, as in Ireland formerly, by brutal coercion, the answer of violence to violence is justified and inevitable.'[1]

This passage makes crystal clear Sri Aurobindo's view regarding the use of violence in the national struggle. There is no question of his condemning violent means, though as a tactical step he might advocate other approaches. When the Mother is being ruthlessly exploited and oppressed, when her honour and glory are being ground to the dust, how can the children have any nice moral scruples regarding the means to deliver her from her agony. If they are true devotees of the Mother they must strike with *Kshatriya* courage,[2] not deeming any sacrifice too great for her deliverance. Thus it is clear that Sri Aurobindo's approach to the question of violence is in perfect consonance with his theory of the nation and nationalism studied in previous chapters.

---

[1] *The Doctrine of Passive Resistance*, pp. 29-31.

[2] See also *Doctrine of Passive Resistance*, p. 88: 'The sword of the warrior is as necessary to the fulfilment of justice and righteousness as the holiness of the saint. *Rāmdās* is not complete without *Shivaji*. To maintain justice and prevent the strong from despoiling, and the weak from being oppressed, is the function for which the *Kshatriya* was created.'

Direct revolutionary activity falls broadly into two categories, organized armed revolt and individual acts of assassination and terrorism directed against the foreign rulers and their indigenous henchmen. There is little doubt that in the earlier stages Sri Aurobindo did feel that the organization of a successful armed revolt against the British was within the realms of possibility. This is borne out by the view expressed by him in these words:

'At that time the military organization of the great empires and their means of military action were not so overwhelming and apparently irresistible as they now are: the rifle was still the decisive weapon, air power had not yet been developed and the force of artillery was not so devastating as it afterwards became. India was disarmed, but Sri Aurobindo thought that with proper organization and help from outside this difficulty might be overcome, and with the smallness of the regular British armies even a guerrilla warfare accompanied by general resistance and revolt might be effective. There was also the possibility of a general revolt in the Indian Army.'[1]

The celebrated *Bhavāni Mandir* scheme, written and circulated by Sri Aurobindo in 1905, also presupposed the possibility of a mass armed revolt against the British. This pamphlet shows the marked influence of Bankim Chandra Chatterjee's *Ānand Math* on Sri Aurobindo. The scheme envisages a temple to be erected in a secret place among the hills consecrated to the Goddess *Bhavāni*, symbolizing Mother India. In this temple would be founded a new order of *Bramhachārins*, young ascetics who would be consecrated body and soul to the liberation of the Mother from the foreign yoke, and who would spearhead a national spiritual regeneration and the armed struggle for independence. Though the scheme did not materialize, it throws considerable light upon the working of Sri Aurobindo's mind, particularly his view that an armed revolt was feasible if necessary organizational steps were carefully taken. Referring to the *Bhavāni Mandir* pamphlet the Rowlatt Committee Report[2] says that 'the book is a remarkable instance of the perversion of religious ideals to political purposes', and expresses the view

---

[1] *Sri Aurobindo on Himself and on the Mother*, pp. 38-39.

[2] Popularly so known, actually the Report of the Sedition Committee (1918) presided over by the Hon'ble Mr Justice Rowlatt.

that it 'really contains the germs of the Hindu revolutionary movement in Bengal'.[1]

Sri Aurobindo had no illusions, however, about the task which he had set himself. For the disunited, largely apathetic and unorganized Indian people to challenge the might of the most powerful Empire the world had ever seen was no easy task. In fact it seems clear that despite his desire for an armed revolt Sri Aurobindo soon realized that other methods would have to be used to oust the British. Nevertheless, all through the critical years following the partition of Bengal, when Sri Aurobindo emerged as a leader and spokesman of the Nationalist Party, he never lost touch with the underground revolutionary movement which continued to exist in Bengal despite severe British repression. His brother Barindra Ghosh, as we saw in the chapter on the Baroda period, had established the closest links with the secret revolutionary groups functioning mainly in Bengal and Maharashtra. He acted in fact as Sri Aurobindo's contact man with these groups, even when ostensibly Sri Aurobindo was carrying on legal, open political activities.[2] The C.I.D. Department was in fact convinced that Sri Aurobindo masterminded the secret terrorist activities, but they were unable to prove it despite desperate attempts to do so. Thus the prosecution in the

---

[1] Professor P. C. Chakravarty, in an article entitled 'Sri Aurobindo and the Indian Freedom Movement' (Loving Homage, pp. 270-297) rightly remarks that 'In fact what Sri Aurobindo really attempted through the Bhavāni Mandir was not to pervert religious ideals to political purposes, but to transform patriotism into a religion and to provide a spiritual foundation for our political struggle. He was convinced that the goal he had in view could not be achieved by a mere group of leisurely politicians and speech-makers; it could be attained only by a band of political sanyāsins, who would completely dedicate themselves to the service of the Motherland, suffer, and, when necessary, sacrifice themselves in her cause.'

[2] This was confirmed by a meeting I had with Barindra Ghosh in Calcutta in 1959, a few months before his death. In a note on the subject which he gave me he writes: 'Sri Aurobindo not only made organized efforts on constitutional lines to win Swarāj through Swadeshi and boycott of foreign goods and practice of passive resistance including non-payment of taxes if necessary, but he organized also secret societies all over Bengal to violently oust the Imperial power through armed resistance and murder of British officers and judiciary. No way for achievement of the main object was abhorrent or unwelcome to him. Except the C.I.D. Department, none in the country knew that Sri Aurobindo was the inspirer or leader of the Secret Party of Violence too. B. C. Chatterjee was surprised to know that fact from me and was persuaded with difficulty to admit the indisputable truth of it.'

Alipur Bomb conspiracy case moved heaven and earth to prove Sri Aurobindo's complicity, but were unable to do so.

In his articles in the *Bande Mātaram* and the *Karmayogin* during the exciting years from 1905 to 1910, Sri Aurobindo took a firm and clear line regarding the use of violence in the nationalist movement. While he deprecated the circumstances which forced young Indians to resort to acts of terrorism[1] and indeed realized clearly that it was absurd to expect random acts of assassination to bring about the country's freedom,[2] he put the blame for these activities fairly and squarely on the shoulders of the British rulers. Again and again he spoke out in clear and fearless terms, accusing the British of fostering and encouraging such clandestine terroristic activities by their shortsighted policy of suppressing and gagging all avenues of peaceful political activity. Thus he writes: 'It is obvious that to attempt to meet secret conspiracy by prohibiting public agitation is a remedy open to the charge of absurdity. The secret conspirator rejoices in silence, the Terrorist finds his opportunity in darkness. Is not the liberty of free speech and free writing denied to the Russian people by more rigorous penalties, a more effective espionage, a far more absolute police rule than any that can be attempted in India? Yet where do the bomb and the revolver, the Terrorist and the secret conspirator flourish more than in Russia?'[3]

His references to the terrorist youths arrested and often executed by the Government reflect clearly his view that they were to be admired for their patriotic fervour and the spirit of sacrifice with which they were imbued. By no means would he accept the official view that they were dangerous criminals who constituted a menace to civilized society. On the contrary he blamed the criminal futility and stupidity of the Government's policy of repression, a 'rank and noxious' policy of which the fruits could not be anything but disastrous. It is also clear that Sri Aurobindo had great personal influence over some of the chief terrorists, including his daring brother Barindra. Professors Haridas and Uma Mukherjee, who have made a close

[1] E. G. *Karmayogin*, 27.11.1909. Writing on 'The Alipur Judgment'.

[2] See *Karmayogin*, 21.8.1909, article entitled 'The Power that uplifts', he says, 'The prolongation of terrorism is undesirable in the interests of the country, for, so long as young men are attached to these methods of violence, the efforts of a more orderly though not less strenuous nationalism to organize and spread itself must be seriously hampered.'

[3] *Karmayogin*, 22.1.1910, 'The New Policy'.

study of the birth and growth of extremist politics in India at the turn of the century, write:

'But even within the left camp further extremism developed by 1906 and it was taking the shape of terrorism. Of this new school in Bengal Aurobindo was in a sense the spiritual father whose influence on Bhupendra Nath Datta and Barindra Kumar Ghose was unmistakable. Bhupendrannath and Barindra Kumar were upholders of the cult of triumph through terror.'[1]

To sum up, therefore, we may say that the use of force to liberate the motherland was an important part of Sri Aurobindo's political technique. Though he toyed with the idea of a mass armed revolt this did not materialize, but he maintained close liaison with revolutionary groups right up to his withdrawal from active politics in 1910. He thus lived a double political life; on the one hand he was an outspoken leader of the Nationalist Party whose creed he eloquently and effectively advocated through press and platform; on the other he was the secret leader and inspirer of the violent, underground terrorist movement designed utterly to demoralize the British. Both these aspects of his political functioning were directed towards the supreme ideal to which he dedicated his life—the liberation and emancipation of Mother India from foreign rule.

[1] *The Origins of the National Education Movement*, p. 74.

13

PASSIVE RESISTANCE AND BOYCOTT

BEFORE proceeding to analyse Sri Aurobindo's views on passive resistance and boycott, it will be helpful to place the matter in its historical perspective and take a brief look at the political developments that led to the birth and growth of this great movement of national protest against British rule. The boycott movement that swept Bengal and had its repercussions in other parts of India can directly be traced to the ill-fated partition of the Province in 1905 by Lord Curzon, who forced the measure down the throat of the Bengalis despite their widespread and vociferous opposition. It is not necessary here to go into the protracted controversy that has raged with regard to the merits of this step. The apologists of Lord Curzon, such as his official biographer Ronaldshay,[1] hold that the measure was amply justified by the fact that the existing Province of Bengal was extremely unwieldy and utterly unsuited to efficient administration. According to this view, Lord Curzon was impelled solely by the desire to promote the interests and happiness of the Bengali people by creating more efficient administrative units which could better look after their interests. Curzon himself undertook a tour of East Bengal in 1904 and tried to explain to the people the advantages of partition, and in his speeches he also stressed the argument of administrative efficiency. Thus in one speech he declared 'Efficiency of administration is, in my view, a synonym for the contentment of the governed. It is the one means of affecting the people in their homes and of adding only an atom perhaps, but still an atom to the happiness of the masses.'[2] As a corollary, Curzon contemptuously dismissed the outcry that had greeted the partition scheme from the time it was just made public in the Risley letter[1] as artificial and based merely on sentiment.

---

[1] *Life of Lord Curzon*, Vol. II, Ch. 24.
[2] *Ibid*, Vol. II, p. 328.

On the other hand there is the view, held and expressed at the time by leading Nationalist figures in Bengal and elsewhere, and even by many Moderate leaders, that the partition was a sinister, māla fīde and utterly unscrupulous move. It was seen as an attempt to destroy the growing national consciousness, spearheaded by Bengal, by permanently weakening the Bengalis and driving a wedge between the two great communities, the Hindus and the Muslims, who inhabited the Province in almost equal proportions. Public opinion manifested itself in a manner unprecedented till then in the annals of British rule in India, and the whole Province rose in violent indignation against the scheme.[2] Despite all this vehement protest, the measure was enforced in the teeth of public opposition. Surendranath Banerjee, the great nationalist leader, well expressed the popular reaction when he wrote:

'The announcement fell like a bomb-shell upon an astonished public. . . . We felt that we had been insulted, humiliated and tricked. We felt that the whole of our future was at stake, and that it was a deliberate blow aimed at the growing solidarity and self-consciousness of the Bengalee-speaking population. Originally intended to meet administrative requirements, we felt that it had drawn to itself a political flavour and complexion, and if allowed to be passed it would be fatal to our political progress and to that close union between the Hindus and Mohammedans upon which the prospect of Indian advancement so largely depended.'[3]

It was from the depths of this humiliation and anger that there arose in Bengal the first mass movement of national pro-

[1] Letter No. 3678 dated Calcutta, December 3, 1903, issued by H. H. Risley, Secretary to the Government of India, on behalf of his Government to the Chief Secretary, Government of Bengal. This letter, which contained a detailed scheme for the partition of Bengal, was notified in G.O.I. *Gazette*, December 12, 1903.

[2] In their book *India's Fight for Freedom* Professors Haridas and Uma Mukherjee have given an interesting detailed account of the events leading up to the Partition of Bengal, the arguments brought forward by the protagonists as well as the antagonists of the scheme, and the profound public reaction that its implementation evoked. See specially Chapter I, 'The Genesis of Partition and the Anti-Partition Agitation (1901-1905)'. Also see an article by Professor P. C. Chakravarti in the *Modern Review*, April, 1959, entitled 'Genesis of the partition of Bengal (1905)'.

[3] *A Nation in the Making*, pp. 187-88.

test against British rule; a movement that threw up some of India's greatest leaders and brought Sri Aurobindo himself into the limelight as the prophet of newly resurgent nationalism; a movement that set in motion forces which resulted within hardly four decades in India attaining its freedom. This is a study of political thought, not political history, and we must resist the temptation to detail the course of the movement, to point out how in five short years it utterly transformed the Indian national movement from a fashionable intellectual pastime into a fervent mass struggle; how it enthused millions and prompted them to heroic acts of courage and self-sacrifice; how, in short, it laid the foundations upon which the imposing structure of Indian freedom was subsequently reared.

Sri Aurobindo had so far been functioning mainly in the background, and not very many people outside his immediate circle were fully aware of the scope and depth of his activities. The partition of Bengal and the subsequent anti-partition agitation that swept the province, however, forced him into the limelight. He was at the time still formally Vice-Principal of the Baroda College, though in fact he spent a good deal of time directing the underground movement in Bengal. In 1906 he took a year's leave without pay from the College and went to Calcutta, which continued to be his headquarters until he left for Chandernagore in February, 1910. It was in these short years that Sri Aurobindo wrote profusely on the theory and practice of Passive Resistance.

As we have seen in the previous chapter, Sri Aurobindo had no hesitation in using violent means to achieve his country's freedom from foreign oppression. He was, however, by no means an impractical dreamer. It appears he soon realized that an armed revolt at that stage of India's history was not feasible, and though he continued to support and guide the underground terrorist movement in the hope that it would demoralize British serving in India, he could have had no illusions as to the possibility of mere terrorism securing the country's freedom.[1] In fact his writings make it clear that in the light of the massive up-

---

[1] E.G. In an article entitled 'The Power that uplifts' (*Karma Yogin*, 21.8.1909) discussing the great Italian leader Mazzini's plans for a series of petty local insurrections he says, 'It seems almost as futile as the idea of some wild brains, if indeed the idea be really cherished, that by random assassination the freedom of this country can be vindicated'.

heaval of public protest as the result of the partition, he wished
the national movement to be not merely an affair of secret
societies and clandestine activities[1] but a broad, open, sweeping
movement which would enthuse and organize the vast Indian
masses in an irresistible upsurge towards emancipation and independence. Thus, although violent methods may have their
place in Sri Aurobindo's technique, his vision and foresight led
him to advocate an entirely different method which he rightly
thought was 'the most natural and suitable weapon' under the
circumstances, whereby the nation could achieve its liberty—
the method of passive resistance. In his writings he often calls it
'defensive resistance', but for the sake of clarity the former expression has been adhered to in the following exposition.

In the *Bande Mātaram* Sri Aurobindo wrote a series of articles
on passive resistance from April 9 to April 23, 1907. These
have been collectively published under the title of *The Doctrine
of Passive Resistance*,[2] and they throw a flood of light upon this
important concept in Sri Aurobindo's political thought. Drawing the distinction between passive and active resistance, Sri
Aurobindo writes: 'The essential difference between passive or
defensive, and active or aggressive, resistance is this, that while
the method of the aggressive resister is to do something by
which he can bring about positive harm to the Government, the
method of the passive resister is to abstain from doing something
by which he would be helping the Government. The object in
both cases is the same—to force the hands of the Government;
the line of attack is different. The passive method is especially
suitable to countries where the Government depends mainly for
the continuance of its administration on the voluntary help and
acquiescence of the subject people.'[3]

From this premise Sri Aurobindo unerringly grasped the idea
that if only this help and acquiescence could systematically be
withdrawn on a national scale, the continuance of British rule
in India would become extremely difficult.[4] Here was a weapon

[1] 'We cannot allow the movement to be driven inward and become an
affair of secret societies and terrorism as it will inevitably become if the
outward expression of it is stopped'—*Bande Mātaram*, weekly edition,
April 12, 1908, on 'The work before us'.
[2] Published by Sri Aurobindo Ashrama, Pondicherry.
[3] *The Doctrine of Passive Resistance*, p. 35.
[4] In his celebrated 'Open Letter to my Countrymen' Sri Aurobindo said:
'Just as "no Representation, no Taxation" was the watchword of American

which would strike at the very root of British power in India and, if wielded with the necessary skill and perseverance, strike a fatal blow. Sri Aurobindo writes: 'The first principle of passive resistance, therefore, which the new school have placed in the forefront of their programme, is to make administration under present conditions impossible by an organized refusal to do anything which shall help either British commerce in the exploitation of the country or British officialdom in the administration of it—unless and until the conditions are changed in the manner and to the extent demanded by the people. This attitude is summed up in one word, boycott.'[1]

To be effective the boycott had obviously to deal with all important aspects of Governmental functioning, and in order to fill the administrative void thus created it was clearly necessary for the nation itself to provide the alternative services. Thus Sri Aurobindo's concept of passive resistance will be dealt with under five broad categories:

(a) Economic boycott and *swadeshi*

(b) Educational boycott and national education

(c) Judicial boycott and national arbitration courts

(d) Executive boycott and national organization

(e) Social boycott.

(a) Economic Boycott and Swadeshi

Probably the first open call in writing for boycott came in the wake of the partition scheme from Krishna Kumar Mitra who, in an editorial published in his weekly paper *Sanjivani* on July 13, 1905, asked the people to renounce foreign goods as

constitutional agitation in the eighteenth century, so "no control, no cooperation" should be the watchword of our lawful agitation—for constitution we have none—in the twentieth'.

[1] *The Doctrine of Passive Resistance*, pp. 35-36. At the time Sri Aurobindo wrote, the term 'Boycott' was barely twenty-five years old. It is defined in the Shorter Oxford Dictionary as follows: 'to combine in refusing to hold relations of any kind with (the other party) on account of political or other differences, so as either to punish him, or coerce him into abandoning his position. The word was first used to describe the action instituted by the Irish Land League towards those who incurred its hostility.' The term arose in 1881 when Captain Boycott, an Irish landlord, was thus ostracized by the Irish agrarian insurgents.

completely as possible under the circumstances.[1] This was
followed by numerous public and private meetings in which the
partition proposal was vehemently attacked and boycott mooted,
culminating in the historic meeting at the Calcutta Town Hall
on August 7, 1905. This was the biggest protest meeting ever
held so far in the annals of British-Indian rule, and was attended
by thousands of people drawn from all walks of life. Revolutionary enthusiasm was also unparalleled. The meeting passed
five resolutions, the third of which became famous in the boycott
resolution. Although its wording was moderate, its effect was
revolutionary and it laid the basis of the great boycott agitation
that subsequently ensued. The resolution ran as follows:

'That this meeting fully sympathizes with the Resolution
adopted at many meetings held in the mofussil, to abstain from
the purchase of British manufactures so long as the partition
Resolution is not withdrawn, as a protest against the indiffer-
ence of the British public in regard to Indian affairs and the consequent disregard of Indian public opinion by the present
Government.'

It is significant to note that though boycott was envisaged as
a temporary measure for the removal of a specific grievance, it
in fact developed into a vital feature of the struggle to throw
off entirely the fetters of British rule. Its tremendous poten-
tiality for damaging the economic interests of the British and
for awakening mass enthusiasm were quickly grasped by astute
minds. Sri Aurobindo soon became an ardent advocate of boycott, and in his writings we find an incisive theoretical analysis
of its importance and also valuable hints regarding its technique.
Later, of course, Mahatma Gandhi developed boycott-*swadeshi*
into a potent weapon in the struggle against the British, but it
is important to remember that its foundations were firmly laid
at least a decade before he came on the Indian political scene.

---

[1] *India's Fight for Freedom* (Mukherjees), p. 33. In a footnote the authors
add 'From the I.B. Records, West Bengal Government, L. No. 476/193 we
learn that the idea of boycott of British goods for the redress of political or
economic grievances of the people had been growing in Bengal ever since
the last quarter of the nineteenth century, and that immediately before the
formal beginning of the Boycott-Swadeshi Movement (August 7, 1905), it
was Tahal Ram Ganga Ram who early in 1905 vigorously preached the idea
of boycott in the course of his impassioned speeches at Calcutta'.

Sri Aurobindo laid out the rationale of economic boycott in the following words:

'We are dissatisfied with the fiscal and economic conditions of British rule in India, with the foreign exploitation of the country, the continual bleeding of its resources, the chronic famine and rapid impoverishment which result, the refusal of the Government to protect the people and their industries. Accordingly we refuse to help the process of exploitation and impoverishment in our capacity as consumers, we refuse henceforth to purchase foreign and especially British goods or to condone their purchase by others. By an organized and relentless boycott of British goods, we propose to render the further exploitation of the country impossible.'[1]

The theory was thus based on two major assumptions, both of them correct. The first was that the essence of British rule in India lay in its economic exploitation of the country. This is, of course, now universally accepted. The British first came to India as a trading class, and in fact the early political exploits of the East India Company were engendered by its desire to safeguard its economic interests. Even after the political control of Indian affairs had passed from the Company to the British Government, the aspect of economic exploitation was always predominant. The 'nation of shopkeepers' found in India an ideal storehouse of cheap raw material and a growing market for British manufactured finished goods, and they exploited the situation with ruthless efficiency. The second assumption behind the boycott theory was that if a determined, patriotic effort was made by freedom-loving Indians they could voluntarily abstain from the purchase and use of British-manufactured goods, and that if this could be done in a sustained manner on a large enough scale, it would strike a deadly blow at British power in India. This was also proved correct by the course of future events. The boycott movement within a few months spread like wild fire throughout the Province, eliciting the enthusiastic support of all sections of the people, including Muslims, and specially evoking mass participation of students. The movement brought together some of the greatest leaders of Bengal, men like Ashvini Kumar Dutt, Surendra Nath Bannerjee, Rabindranath Tagore, Dwijendralal Roy, Bipin Chandra Pal, Ananda Chandra Roy,

[1] *Doctrine of Passive Resistance*, pp. 36-37.

Abdul Rasul, Maulvi Liaquat Hassain and numerous others.[1]

Sri Aurobindo, through the columns of the *Bande Mātaram*, kept up a constant stream of invigorating and inspiring comment on the movement. He saw in the boycott movement a potent weapon whereby it might be possible for India to shake off British rule without a bloody revolution. Thus he writes:

'We must always remember in this connection that alien absolutism in this country depends helplessly on the co-operation of our own people. Let that co-operation be withdrawn and bureaucratic absolutism tumbles in like a house of cards. A very old discovery this, but it is only now that India seems to be within a measurable distance of actively grasping its significance. And it is this necessity of indigenous help that renders a bloodless passage to liberty in India perhaps possible.'[2]

Again in one of his speeches, he said:

'On their fidelity to *swadeshi*, to boycott, to passive resistance rested the hope of a peaceful and spiritual salvation. On that depended whether India would give the example, unprecedented in history, of a revolution worked out by moral force and peaceful pressure.'[3]

Boycott, as we have seen, involves abstaining from the purchase of foreign goods. But it does not, and cannot, mean that the people should cease for ever from consuming goods at present manufactured abroad. The logical corollary of boycott, therefore, is *swadeshi*, the manufacture in one's own country of all the goods that the people require. This obviously cannot be done overnight, in fact it is a long and slow process, but the ideal of economic self-sufficiency is an essential counterpart to the theory of boycott. As Sri Aurobindo put it 'If we refuse to supply our needs from foreign sources, we must obviously supply them ourselves; we cannot have the industrial boycott without *swadeshi* and the expansion of indigenous industries.'[4]

Boycott thus had two great objectives. The first was to shake

[1] *India's Fight for Freedom* (Mukherjees) gives in detail the fascinating story of the march of the movement during the crucial years 1905-6.

[2] *Bande Mataram* weekly edition, September 29, 1907. 'Bureaucracy and Nationalism'.

[3] Report of Mukartuli Speech—*Speeches* (Sri Aurobindo), p. 136.

[4] *The Doctrine of Passive Resistance*, p. 39.

the foundations of British power in India; the second to bring about a rapid growth in indigenous industries for producing in India goods required by its people, thus setting in motion forces that would inevitably bring about the economic resurgence of the nation. In his writings Sri Aurobindo always laid stress upon both aspects. For him they were the two sides of the same coin, boycott the negative side and *swadeshi* the positive. Thus he writes: 'The first condition of a successful boycott, therefore, is the organization of national industry with a view, first, to the improvement and extension of that which exists, secondly, to the opening up of new lines of enterprise.'[1] Conversely, he argues that 'Boycott of foreign goods is a necessary condition for the encouragement of *swadeshi* industries. . . .'[2] There is no contradiction here, merely the intention to stress the fact that boycott and *swadeshi* are inextricably correlated, and that the one without the other was doomed to failure.

In fact the boycott-*swadeshi* movement did lead to a remarkable spurt in indigenous industry, specially in such fields as textiles where bonfires of Manchester and Lancashire cloth became a common sight throughout the country, particularly in Bengal and Maharashtra.[3] A detailed review of the growth of indigenous industry in India, both large-scale and cottage, in the first decade of this century lies outside the scope of this work. Here it is necessary merely to point out that in Sri Aurobindo's political technique the concepts of boycott and *swadeshi* were closely connected, and he saw clearly that it was only if both were successful that full political advantage would be forthcoming in the national struggle against foreign domination.

---

[1] *The Karmayogin*, January 8, 1910. A practical boycott.

[2] 'An Open Letter to My Countrymen'.

[3] In *India's Fight for Freedom* (Mukherjees) the authors say: '*Swadeshi* movement, being at once a patriotic and an economic movement, gave a mighty stimulus not only to our political aspirations but also to the industrial regeneration of the country. The weaving industry of India in particular received the greatest impetus from the *swadeshi* movement. By a systematic and relentless boycott of British cloths and by fostering and stimulating a temper for things *swadeshi*, the national movement of 1905 created in the country a tremendous demand for indigenous articles. As the demand for indigenous cloths grew, increasing attempts were made to start new mills. The first Indian Industrial Conference held at Banaras in December, 1905, with Mr R. C. Dutt as the President, was a very significant step in the direction of focussing public attention on the immense prospects and possibilities of native industries and succeeded in inspiring their minds along the lines of constructive *swadeshi*'. pp. 126-27.

H

(b) Educational boycott and national education

The contours of national consciousness are formed as the result of centuries of history and tradition, and represent the accumulated wisdom and experience of the race. But it has been abundantly proved that this consciousness is greatly influenced by the prevalent system of education imparted to the youth of the nation. The introduction in India of the British system of education is an outstanding case in point. It has been correctly said that 'No single act of British policy has had a more lasting influence on the evolution of modern Indian thought than the decision in 1835 to use governmental funds to support education in the English language and to adopt the curriculum prevalent in English schools.'[1] This is not the place to study the fascinating history of the controversy between the 'Orientalists' and the 'Anglicists' on the Committee on Public Instruction which preceded this decision. It must suffice to say that the former, led by T. B. Macaulay and ably supported by the views of Raja Rammohan Roy,[2] ultimately emerged successful and the decision to introduce English education was taken. Even to outline the profound social and political effects that flowed from this decision would require volumes. It would not be incorrect to say that modern India would have been different in almost every respect if the decision had not been taken. As the masterly commentary in the Sources of Indian Tradition sums it up:

'The introduction of this system of education had two main results. On the one hand it greatly accelerated the diffusion of Western ideas and the Western outlook on life among Indian intellectuals. On the other hand, both the rapid penetration of foreign ways and attitudes, and the publication of the Hindu classics in English translation stimulated movements defending Hinduism or demanding greater political opportunities for Indians—movements whose leaders often wrote, spoke and

---

[1] Sources of Indian Tradition (Columbia), p. 587-88. It is true that as early as 1813 the British Parliament passed the following orders to the East India Company when its licence was renewed. 'That a sum of not less than a lac of rupees, in each year, shall be set apart, and applied to the revival and improvement of literature, and the encouragement of the learned natives of India and for the introduction and promotion of knowledge of the sciences among the British territories in India.' This sum, however, was expended mainly on Sanskrit and Arabic schools.

[2] See his letter on Education addressed to the Governor-General Lord Amtherst in 1823 (English Works, pp. 471-74).

thought in English. . . . English education produced another drastic change in the Indian environment. By providing a common language and a common cultural background for men in all parts of India previously separated by linguistic, regional and cultural differences, it offered Indians the opportunity of creating a common, modern culture of their own. It was only a question of time until these new conditions of all-Indian unity gave birth to political self-consciousness and to Indian Nationalism itself."[1]

Despite the great advantages that India derived, and continues to derive, from English education, there is no doubt that the curricula and type of education introduced had some glaring defects. The avowed aim of Macaulay was to produce a class of 'interpreters', of babus who would assist the British in the task of governing the vast Indian masses.[2] As such, the curricula was excessively formalistic, void of any integral relationship with the social and economic life of India, excessively examination and degree orientated, and far removed from the spiritual and cultural milieu of India. This caused growing resentment and opposition among the increasingly self-conscious section of the Indian intelligentsia, particularly in Bengal. The opposition crystallized in the regime of Lord Curzon when in 1902 the Indian Universities Commission published its *Report* along with a note of dissent by Gooroo Das Banerjee, its only Hindu member. On the basis of this majority report the Government passed in 1904 the Indian Universities Act. The whole public controversy which surrounded the Report and the Act led to a keen spurt in public interest regarding the problem of education, and to the establishment in 1902 of the 'Dawn Society' by Satish Chandra Mukherjee.[3] The partition of Bengal in 1905

[1] *Sources of Indian Tradition* (Columbia), pp. 588-89.

[2] 'We must at present do our best to form a class who may be interpreters between us and the millions whom we govern'—Macaulay in his celebrated 'Minute on Education', 1835. In all fairness it must be added that other Englishmen, such as Lord Minto, David Hare, and Lord Amherst did have more exalted motives in supporting the introduction of English into Indian education. Many were sincerely convinced of the benefits that would accrue to India by such a step.

[3] In *Origins of the National Education Movement* Professors Haridas and Uma Mukherjee give a highly informative account of Satish Chandra Mukherjee's role in the birth and growth of the movement. They also describe the course of the movement itself in great detail, including the founding of the National Council of Education and Society for the Pro-

marked, as we have seen, an immense and unprecedented up-surge of anti-British feeling and agitation throughout the Province, and the cry of 'boycott' and 'swadeshi' spread like wild fire through the land. This expressed itself as much in the educational field as in any other, and educational boycott became an important plank in the political programme of the new Nationalist party.

Sri Aurobindo, acute political observer as he was, immediately grasped the importance of educational boycott. He saw on the one hand that it was an essential feature of the integrated structure of boycott that he envisaged as a potent weapon in the struggle for national liberation. On the other, he realized that this aspect of boycott would directly effect and enthuse the student community, whose active support would be a great asset to the nationalists in their struggle. In fact both these assumptions were proved true, and in particular the students of Bengal played a heroic part in the crucial years 1905-1910 in spreading the cult of boycott throughout the province despite severe repression and intimidation from the authorities.

Writing on the doctrine of passive resistance, Sri Aurobindo refers to educational boycott and says:

'We are dissatisfied also with the conditions under which education is imparted in this country, its calculated poverty and insufficiency, its anti-national character, its subordination to the Government and the use made of that subordination for the discouragement of patriotism and the inculcation of loyalty. Accordingly we refuse to send our boys to Government schools or to schools aided and controlled by the Government; if this educational boycott is general and well-organized the educational administration of the country will be rendered impossible and the control of its youthful minds pass out of the hands of the foreigner.'[1]

In his position as first Principal of the Bengal National College Sri Aurobindo was closely associated with the movement of national education, although from contemporary

motion of Technical Education in 1905. These two bodies each set up an important educational institution; the former the Bengal National College and School on August 14, 1960, with Sri Aurobindo as its first Principal, and the latter the Bengal Technical Institute on July 25, 1906.

[1] *The Doctrine of Passive Resistance*, p. 37.

reports it is clear that his active role in Nationalist politics did not leave him any time to devote to the details of College administration, and that his association with it was mainly to lend it the prestige of his name.[1] It is clear, however, that educational boycott and national education is an important constituent of Sri Aurobindo's political technique.

(c) *Judicial boycott and national arbitration courts*

'We are dissatisfied with the administration of justice, the ruinous costliness of the civil side, the brutal rigour of its criminal penalties and procedure, its partiality, its frequent subordination to political objects. We refuse accordingly to have any resort to the alien courts of justice, and by an organized judicial boycott propose to make the bureaucratic administration of justice impossible while these conditions continue.'[2] In these words Sri Aurobindo puts forward the concept of judicial boycott which, in his view, was a necessary weapon in the boycott armoury. Consistent with the basic idea of not co-operating with any of the Governmental agencies set up by the foreign rulers, Sri Aurobindo saw that judicial boycott was essential. He realized that legal disputes were a fundamental factor of social life, and for this purpose proposed the setting up of national arbitration courts to try and adjudicate such disputes. He wrote: 'If we decline to enter the alien courts of justice, we must have arbitration courts of our own to settle our disputes and differences.'[3]

There is no doubt regarding the theoretical importance of judicial boycott in Sri Aurobindo's political thought, although in his writings he pays much less attention to this point than to other aspects of passive resistance such as *swadeshi* and national education. In practice also it would seem that judicial boycott never really caught on, and in 1909 even Sri Aurobindo admits that 'The movement of arbitration, successful in its inception,

---

[1] It appears, also, that despite its early promise the movement for national education rapidly lost its momentum by 1910. See Sri Aurobindo's editorial in the *Karmayogin* dated January 1, 1910, on 'National Education', and also *The Origins of the National Educational Movement* (Mukherjees). Sri Aurobindo resigned from the Principalship of the National Council of Education on 2.8.1907 as the managers of the Council wanted to keep it free from political activities.

[2] *The Doctrine of Passive Resistance*, pp. 37-38.

[3] *Ibid*, p. 39.

has been dropped as a result of repression'.[1] Apart from repression, however, there were two other reasons for its failure. The first was the fact that it was not an easy task to set up courts with suitably qualified judges and all the necessary legal paraphernalia. Rough and ready arbitration may be all right in a village dispute, but in the vastly more sophisticated society of a great city like Calcutta it was not easy to get by with such methods. Also, in disputes often involving large sums of money, there was no compulsion for people to resort to other than the duly established courts of law. It was easier to persuade even wealthy people to wear *swadeshi* cloth than to give up established law courts for the doubtful advantage of a national arbitration court.

The second factor which, when seen in perspective outside the heated emotions of that period, clearly militated against the success of the judicial boycott was the remarkable impartiality and integrity of the British system of justice. No doubt there were numerous misuses of judicial power, but by and large it must be said to the credit of the British that the system of justice they established in India was perhaps the fairest that any conqueror has given to a subject people. This is clearly borne out by the fact that on many occasions British judges handed down judgments which struck extremely grave blows at the prestige and interests of the British Government in India. Outstanding among such cases was the judgment by Mr Beachcroft in the celebrated Alipore Bomb Conspiracy Case (1909) in which Sri Aurobindo was acquitted despite the frantic efforts of the British Government to get him sentenced.

In fact, the limitations of judicial boycott were well understood by Sri Aurobindo himself. Writing on 'The Law and the Nationalist' he strictly limits the scope of judicial boycott when he writes:

'We think the Nationalists ought to take every opportunity of testing the extent of the liberties still allowed to us in the ordinary course of the law. We are aware that a section of Nationalist opinion has held that our principle of *swadeshi*-boycott ought to debar us from taking any part in any legal proceedings whatever. While many of us have openly expressed our admiration for the heroic stoicism with which this principle

[1] *Karmayogin*, December 25, 1909, article entitled 'To My Countrymen'.

has been adhered to in many cases, we have not held it binding on any except those fine consciences to whom it appealed, nor would we allow it to guide our own action. We hold that no Nationalist should resort to the British Courts under the present political conditions as against a brother Nationalist or in any circumstances which give him a real choice. If he is dragged to the criminal or civil courts by others he is entitled to defend himself to the end by all the means that the law provides. If arbitration is refused in a case where his interests are attacked, he is absolved from the self-denying obligation, or if the law of the land compels him as a land-holder or propertied business-man to protect himself by certain legal forms it is obvious that he cannot deny himself that protection without imperilling work or wealth necessary to the nation. The same over-riding rule of necessity which compels us to exclude machinery and other instruments of education, work and production from the boycott, limits the application of the arbitration principle and the abstention from British courts."[1]

This passage clearly reveals that Sri Aurobindo realized the serious practical limitations of arbitration and judicial boycott. Although the concept occupies a place in his general theory of boycott, he was realist enough to see and admit that its applica-tion was strictly limited.

(d) Executive boycott and national organization

The executive branch of Government comes into the closest touch with the daily life of its people. While the legislative and judicial functions are very important, they do not possess that constant immediacy of contact with the governed which is the raison d'etre of the executive. It is therefore obvious that if any boycott of a foreign Government is to be successful it must include a boycott of the executive machinery. Sri Aurobindo saw this clearly, and also was fully aware of the fact that a handful of British were able to govern India only with the active or passive co-operation of the Indians themselves. If this link could once be broken, if the Indian co-operation to the British rulers could once effectively be withdrawn, Sri Aurobindo thought that British rule in India would be gravely weakened and in fact ultimately collapse. This was the basic idea behind his theory of boycott, particularly executive boycott.

[1] The Karmayogin, September 4, 1909.

Sri Aurobindo lays down his concept of executive boycott in the following words:

'We disapprove of the executive administration, its arbitrariness, its meddling and inquisitional character, its thoroughness of repression, its misuse of the police for the repression instead of the protection of the people. We refuse, accordingly, to go to the executive for help or advice or protection or to tolerate any paternal interference in our public activities, and by an organized boycott of the executive propose to reduce executive control and interference to a more skeleton of its former self. The bureaucracy depends for the success of its administration on the help of the few and the acquiescence of the many. If the few refused to help, if Indians no longer consented to teach in Government schools or work in Government offices, or serve the alien as police, the administration could not continue for a day. We will suppose the bureaucracy able to fill their places by Eurasians, aliens or traitors; even then the refusal of the many to acquiesce, by the simple process of no longer resorting to Government schools, courts of justice or magistrates' katcherries would put an end to administration.'[1]

This concept brings us to the crucial question of the attitude which the governed should adopt towards laws made by his foreign masters. In most cases of foreign rule, specially where the ultra-legalistic British were involved, there was a complex of laws and regulations which the executive sought to administer. Obviously, any scheme of executive boycott would bring the boycotter into direct clash with the laws of the land. Sri Aurobindo meets this problem head-on. He writes:

'A law imposed by a people on itself has a binding force which cannot be ignored except under extreme necessity: a law imposed from outside has no such moral sanction; its claim to obedience must rest on coercive force or on its own equitable and beneficial character and not on the source from which it proceeds. If it is unjust and oppressive, it may become a duty to disobey it and quietly endure the punishment which the law has provided for its violation.'[2]

This is an unambiguous statement, and shows that in Sri

[1] *The Doctrine of Passive Resistance,* p. 38.
[2] *Ibid,* p. 53.

Aurobindo's political theory there was the clear realization that laws issuing from the fiat of an alien government do not have necessarily a binding force upon the governed.[1] From this he derives two important canons of executive boycott and passive resistance, first, 'that to break an unjust coercive law is not only justifiable but, under given circumstances, a duty',[2] and second, 'that to resist an unjust coercive order or interference is not only justifiable but, under given circumstances, a duty.'[3]

It is well known that among all forms of executive boycott the non-payment of taxes is traditionally the most popular and, if successfully achieved, the most effective. Sri Aurobindo did not include this as one of the immediate policies of the national party, because he realized that it was an extreme measure which could only succeed if the people had behind them a strong national organization and, as he put it, 'an ultimatum should never be presented unless one is prepared to follow it up to its last consequences.'[4] Nevertheless, he was fully aware of the importance of a no-tax campaign, for he writes:

'The payment of taxes is the most direct assistance given by the community to the administration and the most visible symbol of acquiescence and approval. To refuse payment is at once the most emphatic protest possible short of taking up arms, and the sort of attack which the administration will feel immediately and keenly and must therefore parry at once either by conciliation or by methods of repression which will give greater vitality and intensity to the opposition. The refusal to pay taxes is a natural and logical result of the attitude of passive resistance.'[5]

We may now turn to the logical corollary of executive boycott and indeed all other forms of boycott, an effective national organization. This is in fact required for the success of the whole Boycott and Passive Resistance Movement, but it is being dealt with here because of its special importance in the context of executive boycott.

It is obvious that in a country as vast and populous as India,

---

[1] In this sense his theory is more akin to the view of Laski than to the classical Austinian concept.

[2] *The Doctrine of Passive Resistance*, p. 53.

[3] *Ibid*, p. 56.

[4] *Ibid*, p. 46.

[5] *The Doctrine of Passive Resistance*, p. 41.

or even the Province of Bengal, no really effective movement against foreign rule—specially such an advanced and sophisticated movement as boycott and passive resistance—could succeed unless it was effectively organized on a national basis. As Sri Aurobindo unerringly realized 'in a vast country like India any such general conflict with dominant authority as is involved in a no-taxes policy needs for its success a close organization linking province to province and district to district, and a powerful central authority representing the single will of the whole nation which alone could fight on equal terms the final struggle of defensive resistance with bureaucratic re-repression.'[1] Throughout his writings, both in the *Bande Mātaram* and the *Karmayogin*, Sri Aurobindo stresses this need for the development of a national authority in India which would 'organize her scattered strengths into a single and irresistible whole'[2] and thus spearhead the triumphant struggle for national liberation.

Sri Aurobindo evidently hoped that such a national organization would be provided by the Congress once it had been purged of the timid 'Moderate' element and re-fashioned by the Nationalists into a new and potent instrument. Thus in his 'An open letter to my countrymen' he says that 'The nationalist programme was to build up a great deliberative and executive organization on the basis of a reconstituted Congress, and this scheme still remains the only feasible means of organizing the country.'[3] Although the nationalists continued to grow in strength, however, they were not able to gain full control of the Congress. In fact the Congress in 1906 finally split between the two groups, with the Government providing all possible aid to the Moderates and using all its powers of intimidation to defeat the Nationalists. Nevertheless, it is significant that it was only when the Congress, under Mahatma Gandhi, did finally create a powerful All-India organization that it was really able to threaten and ultimately dislodge the British power in India. Sri Aurobindo was one of the few early Nationalist leaders clearly to see the importance of a national organization as the pre-

---

[1] *Ibid*, p. 46.

[2] *Bande Mātaram* weekly edition, March 22, 1908, 'The Need of the Moment'.

[3] *Speeches* (Appendix), p. 152.

requisite for the success not only of executive boycott but of the whole national movement itself.

(e) Social Boycott

From the analysis so far it is clear that boycott was for Sri Aurobindo no mere political pastime but a deadly earnest tactic in the struggle for national freedom. As such, it was necessary to devise some sort of sanction which could be used against those Indians who were unpatriotic enough to reject the boycott movement and co-operate with the British to the detriment of the true national interest. In view of the fact that executive power was in the hands of the British themselves, it would be necessary to devise a method which could be used by the people without resorting to any executive fiat. Such a method was the practice of social boycott. As Sri Aurobindo writes:

'The social boycott is a weapon absolutely necessary for the enforcement of the popular will in this matter . . . it consists merely in a passive abstinence from all countenance to the offender—sending him to Coventry, in the English phrase; it is effective and, if properly applied, instantaneously effective . . .'[1]

The idea is basically very simple. The offender is to be shunned socially, in parties, festivals, weddings and so on. He is to be made to feel the scorn and contempt of his fellow-countrymen due to his anti-national activities. A great advantage of the social boycott was that it did not involve any direct clash with the law or resort to violence. Sri Aurobinda stresses this when he writes:

'. . . it involves, as the *Englishman*[2] has been obliged to see, no violence, no disregard of public opinion, no breach of the peace.'[3] And again . . . 'we believe that social boycott involving no violence or direct coercion is perfectly legal, but it is certain that not only the Anglo-Indian community at large but a portion of the judiciary would be glad to find it illegal.'[4]

The latter part of the observation quoted above was certainly

---

[1] The *Karmayogin*, August 14, 1909, 'Social Boycott'.
[2] A contemporary newspaper, owned and run by the British.
[3] The *Karmayogin*, August 14, 1909. 'Social Boycott'.
[4] *Ibid*, September 4, 1909, 'The Law and the Nationalist'.

borne out by events. Several judges did in fact pass judgments which had the effect of making acts of social boycott illegal, for example the Kaul Boycott case.[1] Commenting on the case Sri Aurobindo shows that he had carefully studied the implications of social boycott and was by no means blind to its possible abuses. He writes:

'We are aware of the grave consequences of the misuse of the social boycott to prevent the legitimate exercise by the individual of his free reason and honest conviction. We therefore advocate it only in very serious instances when the whole community is attacked in a vital point and is practically at one in resenting the act as fatally injurious to it.'[2]

Continuing, however, he says:

'Now that the educated classes of the Hindu community are at one in the belief that the swadeshi movement supported by boycott is necessary to the economical existence of their community, to say nothing of the whole nation, they are justified in refusing to have any dealings with those who out of personal and selfish motives deal a blow at that movement by persisting in the purchase of foreign articles.'[3]

Thus we see that in Sri Aurobindo's carefully considered theory of boycott—economic, educational, judicial and executive—the concept of social boycott is an important constituent. In fact it supplies the required coercive factor in the theory, although the 'coercion' does not involve any violence or breach of the law, and thus completes the imposing structure of the boycott technique. As he puts it:

'Wherever passive resistance has been accepted, the necessity of the social boycott has been recognized as its natural concomitant. "Boycott foreign goods and boycott those who use foreign goods" must be accepted by all who are in earnest. For without this boycott of persons the boycott of things cannot be effective; without the social boycott no national authority depending purely on moral pressure can have its decrees effectively

[1] See The Karmayogin, September 4, 1909, on 'The Kaul Judgment', and 'The Implications in the Judgment'.
[2] Ibid, 'The Social Boycott'.
[3] See The Karmayogin, September 4, 1909, 'The Social Boycott'.

executed; and without effective boycott enforced by a strong national authority the new policy cannot succeed."[1]

Before we sum up the political technique expounded by Sri Aurobindo, it will be helpful to mention his ideas regarding the nature of 'passive' or 'defensive' resistance and the place of force therein. The technique of boycott which we have studied in detail was generally expected to be carried on in a peaceful manner. As Sri Aurobindo puts it: 'In a peaceful way we act against the law or the executive, but we passively accept the legal consequences.'[2] But it is clear that this peaceful approach is, in Sri Aurobindo's concept, by no means unconditional. It depends upon the attitude adopted by the Government, and, as we saw in a previous chapter, he had no aversion to the use of force if circumstances so demanded. He makes this very clear when he writes:

'There is a limit however to passive resistance. So long as the action of the executive is peaceful and within the rules of the fight, the passive resister scrupulously maintains his attitude of passivity, but he is not bound to do so a moment beyond. To submit to illegal or violent methods of coercion, to accept outrage and hooliganism as part of the legal procedure of the country, is to be guilty of cowardice, and, by dwarfing national manhood, to sin against the divinity within ourselves and the divinity in our motherland. The moment coercion of this kind is attempted, passive resistance ceases and active resistance becomes a duty. . . . But though no longer passive, it is still a defensive resistance. Nor does resistance pass into the aggressive stage so long as it resists coercive violence in its own kind and confines itself to repelling attack. Even if it takes the offensive, it does not by that mere fact become aggressive resistance unless the amount of aggression exceeds what is necessary to make defence effective. . . . The new politics, therefore, while it favours passive resistance, does not include meek submission to illegal outrage under that term! It has no intention of overstressing the passivity at the expense of the resistance. . . . Passive resistance cannot build up a strong and great nation unless it is masculine, bold and ardent in its spirit and ready at any moment and at the slightest notice to supplement itself with active re-

[1] *The Doctrine of Passive Resistance*, p. 58.
[2] *Ibid*, p. 62.

sistance. We do not want to develop a nation of women who know only to suffer and not how to strike.'[1]

This lengthy quotation has been made in order to stress an important feature in Sri Aurobindo's concept of passive resistance, a feature in which, incidentally, he differs sharply from the subsequent Gandhian doctrine. Sri Aurobindo's desire was above all to infuse into a dormant and cowed nation a new spirit of strength and power, a new awareness of its immense spiritual and material potential. This could not be done by any purely passive doctrine, and so even when he advocated passive resistance he made it absolutely clear that it was not a negative and timid concept which could act as a cloak for cowardice and sluggishness, but a dynamic creed which—as he puts it—'while less bold and aggressive than other methods, calls for perhaps as much heroism of a kind and certainly more universal endurance and suffering.'[2]

To sum up, therefore, we may say that in Sri Aurobindo's political thought a good deal of attention has been paid to the actual technique of political action whereby the advent of national freedom could be hastened. This technique has three broad streams: first, a general campaign for the revival of the national spirit, of pride in India's great cultural heritage and of self-confidence and self-consciousness in the vast Indian masses; second, an underground secret movement of violence and terrorism directed against the alien rulers and their Indian stooges and designed to frighten and demoralize the British rulers and their supporters; and third, a five-pronged boycott movement against the foreigner on the economic, educational, judicial, executive and social fronts, and the corresponding development of indigenous institutions to meet the needs and requirements of the people in place of the foreign institutions. Seldom has any political thinker of calibre devoted so much detailed thought to the actual technique of political action. It is a tribute to Sri Aurobindo's intellect that he did not neglect the practical side of politics, and along with his profound political theory gave to his countrymen a concrete scheme for political action.

[1] *The Doctrine of Passive Resistance*, pp. 62-65.
[2] *Ibid*, p. 31.

14

SRI AUROBINDO'S WITHDRAWAL FROM ACTIVE POLITICS IN 1910

SRI AUROBINDO'S rise as a national leader in the critical years 1905-06 was meteoric. Before this he had been working very much behind the scenes, but the events connected with the partition of Bengal forced him to sever his relations with Baroda and to come into the limelight in Calcutta. With his inspiring articles in the *Bande Mātaram* he became almost overnight a national hero, and the whole of the Bengali intelligentsia waited breathlessly for his stirring pronouncements on current events. His career of active politics, however, lasted barely five years, and his subsequent withdrawal from active politics was as dramatic as his rise to eminence. In fact it is an event that has all the elements of a fascinating riddle, and numerous explanations and theories have been put forward to explain it. As this work is devoted to Sri Aurobindo's political thought we will approach the matter from the angle of his political ideas and see whether they do not produce an acceptable and logical explanation.

Before coming to the events of 1909-10, however, it will be helpful to give a brief survey of the developments that took place within the Congress party in the years immediately following partition; developments in which Sri Aurobindo was closely involved.

The years that followed the partition of Bengal in 1905 were historic years, and for the leaders of the resurgent movement of radical nationalism they were years crowded with action and excitement. The great mass upsurge in Bengal, directed not merely against the partition of the province but against the continuance of British rule itself, electrified the whole of India. Tilak in Maharashtra, Lajpat Rai in the Punjab and other radical leaders rode high on the mounting wave of anti-British resentment that, starting from Bengal, swept across the nation. Inevitably this new development was rapidly reflected in the Congress party. It became clear that the Moderates were being increasingly isolated from the mass of public opinion and that effective leadership had passed into the hands of the Radicals.

In the first flush of indignation and anger at the Bengal partition it almost appeared that the two wings of the Congress would reunite in their opposition to the British. Thus in the session of 1905 the great Moderate leader Gopal Krishna Gokhale presided over the Congress and in his presidential address roundly criticized the partition. He said:

'The question that is uppermost in the minds of us all at this moment is the partition of Bengal . . . a cruel wrong has been inflicted on our Bengali brethren and the whole country has been stirred to the deepest depths of sorrow and resentment, as had never been the case before.'[1]

But the hope of a reconciliation proved to be illusory. Tilak and his followers, including Sri Aurobindo who by now was the acknowledged leader of the Radical Movement in Bengal, wanted to push forward with strong measures against the British, while the Moderate leadership after an initial burst of enthusiasm drew back into their 'mendicant' grooves.

In his Presidential address in 1905 Gokhale had, to the surprise of many, given his support to the swadeshi and boycott movements, and had said that the people of Bengal 'had every justification for the steps they took.' Tilak and his group wanted separate resolutions to be passed on swadeshi and the boycott of foreign goods in order to emphasize their importance, but finally they accepted the Malaviya resolution which inter alia stated that the Congress recorded 'its earnest and emphatic protest against the repressive measures which have been adopted by the authorities in Bengal after the people there had been compelled to resort to the boycott of foreign goods as a last protest, and perhaps the only constitutional and effective means left to them of drawing the attention of the British public to the action of the Government of India in persisting in their determination to partition Bengal in utter disregard of the uni-

[1] Report of the Indian National Congress 1905, Presidential Address.

versal prayers and protests of the people."[1]

The resolution, however, perhaps deliberately left vague whether the Congress did or did not approve of the boycott of foreign goods. Tilak and his group looked upon it as a distinct step forward, and the Radical leaders continued their public agitation for *swadeshi* and boycott. A few months later Aurobindo, Bipin Chandra Pal and others from Bengal proposed Tilak's name for the presidentship of the forthcoming Congress at Calcutta. This idea greatly alarmed the Moderates, who countered by cabling to Dadabhai Naoroji in England and inviting him to accept that position. This was an astute move on their part because, as Chirol puts it, 'none could venture openly to oppose him for he was almost the father of the Congress . . . and his high personal character and rectitude of purpose had earned for him universal respect.[2]

The 1906 session of the Congress was attended by 1,663 delegates, one of the largest that had ever been held till then. It passed the celebrated resolution declaring swaraj or self-government to be the goal of the Congress and urging that 'the system of Government obtaining in the self-governing British colonies should be extended to India. . . .'[3] This resolution was passed unanimously, but those on *swadeshi* and boycott gave rise to a heated controversy in the subjects Committee. Finally, however, an open rupture was averted by the 'tact and authority of Dadabhai Naoroji',[4] but the Moderates were forced to agree to three resolutions on boycott, *swadeshi* and national education which clearly reflected the views of the Tilak group. In this session Sri Aurobindo emerged as Tilak's chief lieutenant in Bengal and played a prominent role in discussing and drafting the resolutions.

Although the Radicals were jubilant at having achieved an apparent victory, their joy was tinged with the suspicion that the Moderates might be planning some retrogressive move for the following session. The Moderates on their part were angry and bitter at having had to support the resolutions incorporating the Radical viewpoint. Thus there was no real reconciliation,

---

[1] Report of the Indian National Congress 1905, Resolution XIII.

[2] Valentine Chirol, *Indian Unrest*, p. 51.

[3] Report of the Indian National Congress 1906, Resolution IX, 1908, Presidential Address.

[4] *Ibid.*

I

and both sides prepared for a showdown at the next annual session of the Congress. At the termination of the 1906 session it had been resolved that the next session should be held at Nagpur, but subsequently the Moderate-dominated All-India Congress Committee met in Bombay and changed the venue to Surat. This was an open provocation to the Radicals, who accused the Moderates of doing so because they feared Tilak's following in Nagpur and felt that Surat was safer as it was considered one of the Moderate strongholds.[1] Added to this was the dispute over the election of the President, Lajpat Rai being the Radical candidate and Dr Rash Behari Ghosh the Moderate. Finally Lajpat Rai withdrew to avoid any unpleasantness, but differences between the two groups were sharply aggravated by a report circulated about a week before the session that the Reception Committee had decided to recede from the position taken up by the Calcutta Congress. This report was caused by the non-availability in advance of the draft resolutions and also the fact that the list of headings for subjects likely to be discussed, published a week before the session, did not include the vital subjects of Self-Government, boycott and national education upon which independent resolutions had been passed in 1906.[2]

It was obvious that a showdown was at hand. Tilak, Sri Aurobindo and other Radical leaders made it quite clear before the session began that although they had no desire to split the Congress they would in no case agree to any retreat from the 1906 resolutions. On December 26th the draft resolutions were made available just before the session was to begin, and they revealed that certain changes and modifications had been made in the *swadeshi*, boycott and national education resolutions with a view to watering them down. In the afternoon the session met and there was an uproar over the nomination of the President. The session had to be postponed and it met again the next day.

[1] In *Sri Aurobindo on Himself* we find the following statement: 'The session of the Congress had first been arranged at Nagpur, but Nagpur was predominantly a Marhatta city and violently extremist. Gujerat was at that time predominantly Moderate and Surat was a stronghold of Moderatism . . . So the Moderate leaders decided to hold the Congress at Surat.' pp. 78-79.

[2] See *Indian National Congress—1892-1909* by Dr P. C. Ghosh, Ch. VII. It would appear from contemporary records and reports that the British Government had been severely alarmed by the 1906 resolutions and had determined, through the Moderate leadership, to put a stop to the drift of the Congress towards Radical policies.

It was then that the final debacle was witnessed. Tilak wanted to speak on the election of the President but he was declared out of order. Nevertheless, he came onto the dias and insisted that he be allowed to speak. Suddenly pandemonium broke loose; shoes, chairs and tables began to fly in all directions and many people were injured. The police came into the hall and the meeting broke up in confusion.

This event marked the final split between the Radical and the Moderate wings of the Congress. The Radicals virtually seceded from the organization, leaving the Moderates in sole control.[1] But although for several years the Moderate leaders continued to run the Congress and hold its sessions it became clear that they lacked any mass public support. As Shri R. R. Diwakar puts it:

'The Surat Congress ended in a fiasco but made history. The result was that the Moderates continued to possess the body of the Congress while the spirit went out along with the extremists. For the next ten years Indian nationalism flourished outside the precincts of the National organization. When it returned to the charge in 1916 it completely routed the Moderates, who later continued their existence outside the Congress as a small and not very influential coterie. They ceased to be a political force in the country.[2]

In a way the Surat imbroglio came as a victory for Sri Aurobindo's policy, because it clearly posed the issues between the Moderates and the Extremists in a manner that left no room for ambiguity. It also opened a new avenue of activity for the younger, radical group untrammelled by the retrogressive weight of the Moderate leadership. In fact Sri Aurobindo had all along been urging a clarification of issues such as was brought about at Surat. Before returning to Calcutta, therefore, he decided to respond to invitations from a large number of cities to address them on the radical policy of his group. He visited Baroda, Bombay, Poona, Nasik and Amraoti, and in each

[1] Immediately after the break-up both groups held separate conventions on December 28th. The Moderate Convention was presided over by Rash Behari Ghosh (The Surat Congress and Conferences, India Office Library Tracts 1042, Appendix B 'The Convention') and the Extremist Convention was presided over by Sri Aurobindo (Ibid, Appendix D, 'The meeting of the Extremists').

[2] Mahayogi by R. R. Diwakar, p 69.

place he delivered inspiring speeches and was received with great warmth and enthusiasm.[1]

At this point in our narrative we must return to a fundamental feature of Sri Aurobindo's life, his interest in and active pursuit of Yoga. As we saw in an earlier chapter on the Baroda period, spiritual practices and political activity were from at least as far back as 1900 parallel trends in Sri Aurobindo's life. All through the hectic years of activity during and after the Bengal partition this spiritual activity formed a deep undercurrent to his intense political career. By 1907, however, he felt that he needed some guidance and help on the path, and during his visit to Baroda referred to above he met for the first time one Vishnu Bhaskar Lele, a Maharashtrian Yogi.[2] Though tempting, it is not within the scope of this work to enter into a detailed account of Sri Aurobindo's spiritual practices and experiences at this stage of his life. His biographers refer to them, and he also mentions them in his later writings. A study of political thought must confine itself to the effect of these practices and experiences upon his political life and activity.[3] It is, however, important to mention that Lele agreed to help Sri Aurobindo on condition that 'he would suspend—for Sri Aurobindo was not ready to give up entirely—his political activity.'[4] This he did for three days, during which he sat in meditation under Lele's directions. The results, apparently, were dramatic and quite different from what either Lele or Sri Aurobindo expected. The latter has described the incident in the following words:

'The first result was a series of tremendously powerful experiences and radical changes of consciousness which he (Lele) had never intended—for they were *Advaïtic* and *Vedāntic* and he was against *Advaïta Vedānta*—and which were quite contrary

[1] See *Mahayogi* (Diwakar), p. 70, and *Sri Aurobindo* (K. R. S. Iyengar), pp. 138-144.

[2] See *Mahayogi* (Diwakar), pp. 70-71, *Sri Aurobindo* (Iyengar), p. 138, *Life of Sri Aurobindo* (Purani), pp. 121-122.

[3] As I mentioned in an earlier chapter, we cannot concern ourselves with the objective validity of such experiences. Some will hail them as the first dawning of a mighty spiritual power, others may dismiss them as mere hallucinations. We are concerned with the subjective impact they had upon Sri Aurobindo—his political thought and indeed his whole approach to the question of politics.

[4] *Life of Sri Aurobindo* (Purani), p. 122.

to my own ideas, for they made me see with a stupendous intensity the world as a cinematographic play of vacant forms in the impersonal universality of the Absolute *Bramhan*. The final upshot was that he was made by a Voice within him to hand me over to the Divine within me enjoining an absolute surrender to its will. . . .'[1]

This quotation is important, because it shows that as early as 1907 the spiritual element in Sri Aurobindo's psyche had begun to press to the surface. This began immediately to be reflected in his speeches. In fact soon after meeting Lele in Baroda he proceeded to Bombay where, on January 19, 1908, he addressed a huge public meeting under the auspices of the Bombay National Union. Lele was also present, and asked him to make obeisance to the audience and wait silently for speech to come to him from a source higher than the mind.[2] Sri Aurobindo testified that this is in fact what happened, and indeed that from then onwards he records that inspiration to speak or write always came to him when required from a supramental source. The Bombay speech[3] on 'The present situation' is indeed a remarkable utterance, and shows that the speaker was moved by deep inner compulsions. It was in this speech that he made his famous statement about nationalism being a religion that had come from God, a divine, immortal and invincible religion. In this speech also did he clearly proclaim his conviction that a Divine Power was behind the national movement, a Power that would brook no curbing and would necessarily emerge triumphant. The fact that this eloquent statement of spiritual nationalism came so soon after his experiences with Lele is obviously significant. After his return to Calcutta also his speeches had the same spiritual bias.[4]

In the meantime events in Bengal had been moving rapidly. After the Congress split, in fact probably even before, the Government of India decided to come down with a heavy hand on the Extremists. In 1905 Lord Curzon had been replaced as Viceroy by Lord Minto. The Government started a virulent campaign of forcible suppression of the radical element in Indian

---

[1] Quoted by Purani in *Life of Sri Aurobindo*, pp. 123-24.
[2] See *Sri Aurobindo* (Iyengar), pp. 140-41 and *Mahayogi* (Diwakar), p. 71.
[3] Published in his *Speeches* (Sri Aurobindo Ashrama, Pondicherry), pp. 5-28.
[4] e.g. His speech on April 10, 1908, at Pantis Math, Calcutta, *Sheeches*, pp. 31-33.

politics. So severe was the policy that even Lord Morley, the Secretary of State for India, was constrained on one occasion to address the following words to Lord Minto:

'I must confess to you that I am watching with the deepest concern and dismay the thundering sentences that are being passed for sedition, etc. We must keep order, but excess of severity is not the path to order. On the contrary, it is the path to the bomb.[1]

Brahmabandhab Upadhyaya, Bhupendra Nath Dutt and others were hauled up on the charge of sedition and awarded drastic sentences.[2] The inevitable result was the one clearly foreseen by Morley. Some hot-heads wanted to avenge the death of Upadhyaya by killing Mr Kingsford, the District Judge of Muzaffarpore who had previously ordered the flogging of a young boy in court. On April 10, 1908, two youths threw a bomb at a carriage which they supposed was occupied by Mr Kingsford. In fact the bomb hit and killed two wholly innocent people, the wife and daughter of a Mr Pringle-Kennedy. It was of course a ghastly and unfortunate mistake. As Shyam Sundar wrote a month later in the *Bande Mataram*:

'Outrages of this kind have absolutely no sanction in our ancient tradition and culture. . . .'[3]

Nevertheless, the Government and the Anglo-Indian press completely lost their balance and sense of proportion[4] and hit out

---

[1] Quoted in *Life and Times of C. R. Das*, by P. C. Roy (1927), p. 58 (Footnote).

[2] Upadhyaya, the great Christian nationalist, who through the columns of his paper *Sandhya* played such an important role in arousing radical nationalist feelings in Bengal, died in the Campbell hospital before the case against him could be concluded.

[3] *Bande Mataram*, weekly edition, May 10, 1908.

[4] In *Mahayogi* Shri Diwakar well sums up the reactions to this incident in the following paragraph:
'The Muzaffarpur outrage was the first of its kind in India. Outside the small circle which might have organized it none hailed or admired it. The reactions naturally varied in different quarters. The European Community and the Anglo-Indian press took an alarmist view and called for severe suppression. The younger generation in India looked upon it as a deed of daring, irrespective of its merits or demerits, and was thrilled. The moderate element condemned the whole affair in no uncertain terms. The nationalists too openly repudiated it but did not question the motive and the sacrifice in-

right and left. Police began investigations and soon a miniature bomb factory at Maniktolla was located and seized. A number of people were arrested, including Barindra Kumar Ghosh who was rightly suspected as being the chief organizer behind the whole underground revolutionary movement. It was perhaps natural that Sri Aurobindo should also be suspected of connection with the whole affair, and he was also arrested on the morning of May 4, 1908. All the prisoners were sent to Alipur and lodged there, and soon there began one of the most famous and celebrated trials in Indian history, the Maniktolla Bomb Case, more popularly known as the Alipore Conspiracy Case.

It is not necessary here to give a detailed description of the progress of this famous trial, though it would make a highly interesting narrative.[1] Sri Aurobindo was refused bail, and after several months of preliminary trial the case was finally committed to Sessions on August 19, 1908. The British Government strained every nerve to implicate Sri Aurobindo in the conspiracy, and for this purpose secured the services of the distinguished criminal lawyer Mr Eardley Norton. It therefore became necessary to arrange Sri Aurobindo's defence on an adequate basis, and this task was undertaken by his close friends including his sister Sarojini. She issued an appeal for funds in which she said:

'I know all my countrymen do not hold the same political opinions as he (Sri Aurobindo). But I feel some delicacy in saying that probably there are few Indians who do not appreciate his great attainments, his self-sacrifice, his single-minded devotion to the country's cause, and the high spirituality of his character. These embolden me, a woman, to stand before every son and daughter of India for help to defend a brother—my brother and theirs too.'[2]

The defence was soon taken up by a brilliant rising young lawyer named Chittaranjan Das, later to become famous as the 'Deshabandhu'.[3]

volved. They pointed out that this was a symptom of the mounting desperation of the country and that the Government should take it as a warning and treat it not as a challenge but as a pointer to where their repressive policy was leading.' p. 74.

[1] For a good short account see *Sri Aurobindo* (Iyengar), pp. 154-67.

[2] The *Bande Mataram*, June 13, 1908.

[3] 'Friend of the nation'.

The case dragged on for many months. In the *Life and Times* of C. R. Das[1] we learn that 'in this case 206 witnesses were examined, 4,000 documents were filed and the exhibits, consisting of bombs, revolvers, ammunition, detonators, fuses, poisonous acids and other explosive materials, numbered 5,000'. The District and Sessions Judge trying the case was, by an ironic twist of destiny, one Mr Beachcroft who was at Cambridge with Sri Aurobindo and had stood second to him in Greek![2] Chittaranjan's speech for the defence was spread over eight days and is a masterpiece of forensic eloquence. His final peroration contained his celebrated appeal to the Judge and the two Assessors in the case:

'My appeal to you is this, that long after the controversy will be hushed in silence, long after this turmoil and agitation will have ceased, long after he is dead and gone, he will be looked upon as the poet of patriotism, as the prophet of nationalism and the lover of humanity. Long after he is dead and gone, his words will be echoed and re-echoed, not only in India, but across distant seas and lands. Therefore I say that the man in his position is not only standing before the bar of this court, but before the bar of the High Court of History.'[3]

On April 13, 1909, the two Assessors returned a unanimous verdict of 'not guilty', and about a month later Mr Justice Beachcroft accepted the verdict and acquitted Sri Aurobindo— a tribute alike to the forensic powers of Chittaranjan and the sense of fairness and impartiality deeply engrained in the British system of justice.

This brief description of the Alipore Conspiracy Case has been introduced here for a specific purpose, to form the background for the deep spiritual developments that Sri Aurobindo experienced during that time. In the midst of his active and exciting political activities his arrest and incarceration came as an abrupt shock. He has himself given us an account of his feelings at the

[1] p. 59.

[2] *Sri Aurobindo* (Iyengar), pp. 160-61.

[3] *Life and Times of C. R. Das*, pp. 59-64. One can only wonder at the keen vision of the Deshabandhu whereby he saw clearly that Sri Aurobindo was no ordinary political prisoner but a remarkable person of high destiny.

time in his famous Uttarpara Speech[1] delivered immediately after his acquittal. He said:

'When I was arrested and hurried to the Lal Bazar *Hajāt*,[2] I was shaken in faith for a while, for I could not look into the heart of His intention. Therefore I faltered for a moment and cried out in my heart to Him, "What is this that has happened to me? I believed that I had a mission to work for the people of my country and until that work was done I should have Thy protection. Why then am I here and on such a charge? A day passed and a second day and a third, when a voice came to me from within, 'wait and see'. Then I grew calm and waited; I was taken from Lal Bazar to Alipur and was placed for one month in a solitary cell apart from other men. There I waited day and night for the voice of God within me, to know what He had to say to me, to learn what I had to do. In this seclusion the earliest realization, the first lesson came to me. I remembered then that a month or more before my arrest a call had come to me to put aside all activity, to go into seclusion and to look into myself, so that I might enter into closer communion with Him. I was weak and could not accept the call. My work was very dear to me and in the pride of my heart I thought that unless I was there it would suffer or even fail and cease; therefore I would not leave it. It seemed to me that He spoke to me again and said: 'The bonds you had not the strength to break I have broken for you, because it was not my will nor was it ever my intention that that should continue. I have had another thing for you to do and it is for that I have brought you here, to teach you what you could not learn for yourself and to train you for my work.'

This quotation is intensely revealing. It shows clearly that it was during his confinement in jail that the decisive psychological break with active politics came as the result of a transcending of politics and progression into a deeper and wider sphere of spiritual activity. In jail he read the *Bhagwadgita* and it deeply affected him. As he puts it:

---

[1] *Speeches* (Ashrama), pp. 51-66. Coming as it did immediately after his release, this speech is extremely important for the light it throws upon Sri Aurobindo's spiritual experiences in jail and his subsequent renunciation of active politics.

[2] Lock-up.

'Then He placed the *Gita* in my hands. His strength entered into me and I was able to do the *Sadhana of the Gita*.'[1]

The spiritual development in jail finally culminated in Sri Aurobindo's attaining the mystic experience of the all-pervading Supreme Reality. This is how he describes it:

'I looked at the jail that secluded me from men and it was no longer by its high walls that I was imprisoned; no, it was *Vāsudeva*[2] who surrounded me. I walked under the branches of the tree in front of my cell, but it was not the tree, I knew it was *Vāsudeva*, it was *Sri Krishna* whom I saw standing there and holding over me His shade. I looked at the bars of my cell, the very grating that did duty for a door, and again I saw *Vāsudeva*. It was *Nārayana*[3] who was guarding and standing sentry over me. Or I lay on the coarse blankets that were given to me for a couch and felt the arm of *Sri Krishna* around me, the arms of my Friend and Lover. . . . I looked and it was not the Magistrate whom I saw . . . it was not the Counsel for the prosecution that I saw; it was *Sri Krishna* who sat there . . . and smiled "Now do you fear." He said, "I am in all men and I overrule their actions and their words. . . . I am guiding, therefore fear not. Turn to your own work for which I have brought you to jail and when you come out, remember never to fear, never to hesitate. Remember that it is I who am doing this, not you nor any other. . . . I am the nation and its uprising and I am *Vāsudeva*, I am *Nārayana*, and what I will, shall be, not what others will What I chose to bring about, no human power can stay."'[4]

From these quotations, and other utterances of his after release from jail, it is clear that during his imprisonment he had undergone a profound spiritual experience and transformation. He had always been spiritually inclined, but he emerged from the Alipur jail with the firm conviction that he was merely an instrument in the hands of the Divine, and that the Divine power was intimately and irrevocably working in the national movement, the success of which was therefore assured whether or not he as an individual remained on the scene. This new con-

---

[1] Uttarpara Speech.
[2] The son of Vasudeva, Sri Krishna.
[3] Another name for Lord Krishna.
[4] Uttarpara Speech.

sciousness transformed his approach to the political problems of the day, and soon to the very problem of political activity itself.

During the year in which Sri Aurobindo had remained in detention, the Government had not been inactive. After the Congress split at Surat it had adopted the dual policy of encouraging and patronizing the Moderates while severely repressing the Extremists. This policy was openly advocated by the Moderates. Thus, in his undelivered Presidential Address for the 1907 Session at Surat, Rash Behari Ghosh had remarked that 'if the Government can only rally the Moderates to their side . . . they will extinguish the new party completely, and the ominous shadow which has projected itself over the future fortunes of the country will disappear'. In pursuance of this policy a large number of Extremist leaders had been arrested and sentenced to severe terms of imprisonment, while several, including Tilak, had been deported. Thus when Sri Aurobindo came out of jail there had been a twofold change. On the one hand he himself had changed considerably as the result of his spiritual experiences in jail. On the other hand the India into which he stepped had also changed. Sri Aurobindo himself spoke of this at Uttarpara when he said:

'Now that I have come out I find all changed. One who always sat by my side[1] and was associated with my work is a prisoner in Burma, another[2] is in the North rotting in detention. I looked around when I came out. I looked round for those to whom I had been accustomed to look for counsel and inspiration. I did not find them. There was more than that. When I went to jail, the whole country was alive with the hope of a nation, the hope of millions of men who had newly risen out of degradation. When I came out of jail I listened for that cry, but there was instead a silence. A hush had fallen on the country and men seemed bewildered; for instead of God's bright heaven full of the vision of the future that had been before us, there seemed to be overhead a leaden sky from which human thunders and lightnings rained.'[3]

This was indeed a dismal prospect, and one sufficient to cow even a strong man and break his faith. The fact that it did neither, that Sri Aurobindo rallied to the charge and once more plunged

---

[1] Referring to Tilak, who had been deported to Mandalay in Burma.
[2] Referring to Lala Lajpat Rai.
[3] Uttarpara Speech.

into deep political activity, is a convincing answer to some who hold that he left active politics due to frustration or even fear. His was not a spirit so easily shaken, and his year's stay in jail —Ashramvas,[1] as one of his biographers calls it—had given him added powers of endurance and further strengthened his faith. This is very clear from his subsequent statements and actions. In the very speech from which we have just quoted he goes on to say: 'But one thing I knew, that as it was the Almighty Power of God which had raised that cry, that hope, so it was the same Power which had sent down that silence . . . so that the nation might draw back for a moment and look into itself and know His will. I have not been disheartened by that silence. . . .'[2] And in another speech delivered a few days later at Jhālakati[3] he said: 'But it is a strange idea, a foolish idea, which men have indeed always cherished under such circumstances but which has been disproved over and over again in history— to think that a nation which has once risen, has once been called up by the voice of God to rise, will be stopped by mere physical repression. It has never so happened in the history of a nation, nor will it so happen in the history of India.' These are not the words of a man who is disheartened or discouraged. And, from his deeper spiritual standpoint, Sri Aurobindo proceeded to analyse the causes of the disaster that has overtaken the nationalist movement and saw even in this the hidden, beneficent hand of the Divine. He said in the same speech: 'We were building an edifice to be the temple of our Mother's worship[4]—were rearing her a new and fair mansion, a place fit for her dwelling. It was then that He came down upon us. He flung himself upon the buildings we had raised. He shook the roof with his mighty hands and part of the building was displaced and ruined. Why has He done this? Repression is nothing but the hammer of God that is beating us into shape so that we may be moulded into a mighty nation and an instrument for his work in the world. We are iron upon his anvil and the blows are showering upon us not to destroy but to recreate. Without suffering there can be no growth.' Stirring

---

[1] Iyengar in *Sri Aurobindo*, Chapter ten. The word means 'abode in a hermitage'.

[2] Uttarpara Speech.

[3] *Speeches* (Ashrama), pp. 74-89.

[4] Cf. his *Bhawani* Mandir scheme referred to on page 101.

words indeed, which amply prove the invincible courage and determination of Sri Aurobindo in the face even of the most depressing and adverse circumstances. To suggest that such a man left active politics due to fear or frustration can only be termed absurd and perverse.

Nor were Sri Aurobindo's activities after his release confined merely to delivering eloquent speeches. In fact he launched upon one of the most important and impressive journalistic enterprises of the decade—the publication of two weekly papers, the *Karmayogin* in English and the *Dharma* in Bengali. The first issue of the *Karmayogin* came out in June 19, 1909, within a few weeks of his release from jail. The cover illustration was of Sri Krishna driving Arjuna's chariot, and the motto of the journal was the famous Gita aphorism *Yoga karmasu kaushalam*—Yoga is skill in works. In the opening editorial on 'Ourselves' Sri Aurobindo sketched the policy of the journal in these words:

'The *Karmayogin* will be more of a national review than a weekly newspaper. We shall notice current events only as they evidence, help, affect or resist the growth of national life and the development of the Soul of the nation. Political and social problems we shall deal with from this standpoint, seeking first their spiritual roots and inner causes and then proceeding to measures and remedies. In a similar spirit we shall deal with all sources of national strength in the past and in the present, seeking to bring them home to all comprehensions and make them applicable to our life, dynamic and not static, creative and not merely preservative. For if there is no creation, there must be disintegration; if there is no advance and victory, there must be recoil and defeat.'

The *Karmayogin* was under Sri Aurobindo's editorship for less than eight months, his last issue being dated February 5, 1910. During this period, however, it became the vehicle for some of the most inspired and elevating journalism that India has ever seen. Sri Aurobindo wrote with equal felicity and vigour on a wide spectrum of topics—political, social, economic, cultural, religious and philosophical. His contributions included beautiful English renderings of the Upanishadas and such classics as Kalidāsa's *Ritusamhara* and part of Bankim's *Anana Math*; thoughtful and constructive articles on 'A System of

National Education', 'The Brain of India', 'The National Value of Art' and the masterly series of essays on 'The Ideal of the *Karmayogin*'; and also inspiring and well-informed comment on the various political problems of the day—Indian as well as international. The *Karmayogin* is perhaps unique in the varied galaxy of subjects with which it dealt and the uniformly high standard of language and thought that it maintained, all of which testify to the deep learning and faith of Sri Aurobindo.[1]

Throughout these writings one basic feature is clearly noticeable—a deep spiritual undercurrent which informed his whole approach to the variety of problems with which he dealt. Ever since his release from jail he had been carrying on his spiritual *sādhana*, the fundamental tenet of which was complete sur- render to a higher power and mightier will which he so clearly felt was controlling his actions. There were hints in his speeches and writings that he was contemplating a retirement from active politics. He had realized that his own personal association with the nationalist movement was by no means essential to its success. In fact, in that remarkable document which he called his 'last political will and testament' and which was published in the *Karmayogin* on July 31, 1909, under the title 'An open Letter to my Countrymen'[2] he said:

'All great movements wait for their God-sent leader, the willing channel of His force, and only when he comes more forward triumphantly to their fulfilment. The men who have led hitherto have been strong men of high gifts and commanding genius, great enough to be the protagonists of any other movement, but even they were not sufficient to fulfil one which is the chief current of a world-wide revolution. Therefore the Nationalist party, custodians of the future, must wait for the man who is to come.'[3]

This shows plainly that he had ceased to look upon himself as the destined leader, if in fact he had ever held that view. Indeed

---

[1] I am deeply indebted to my friend Syed Mehdi Imam of the Sri Auro-bindo Ashrama, Pondicherry, for having secured for me from the Ashrama records a large number of hitherto unpublished articles from the *Karma-yogin*. I have made use of this material extensively in the course of the present work.

[2] Published in *Speeches* (Ashrama), pp. 137-154.

[3] Was this, perhaps, a prophetic reference to the emergence a decade later of Gandhiji, who was destined to lead the Nationalists to the final victory?

it is clear that with the spiritual factor in his psyche becoming increasingly predominant the purely political aspect began necessarily to diminish in importance. Thus, while in the *Bande Mātaram* the political outlook had been predominant and the spiritual an undercurrent, in the *Karmayogin* the roles were reversed.

Terrorist outrages were on the increase in 1909 as the Government had succeeded in stifling the Nationalist party, the one political body which offered a legal and peaceful outlet for the people's resentment. Government repression was also on the increase. In the *Karmayogin* Sri Aurobindo commented on the shooting and assassinations, and laid the blame squarely on the Government's repressive policy. Finally he came to the conclusion that as the Nationalists were powerless to stem the rising tide of terrorism sweeping over Bengal, they could only suspend their own strictly lawful and peaceful activities and let the Government deal as best as it could with the situation that its own policies had inexorably created. Thus on February 5, 1910, he wrote in the *Karmayogin*:

'We advise our fellow Nationalists also to stand back and give an unhampered course for a while to Anglo-Indian statesmanship in its endeavours to grapple with this hydra-headed evil.'

His own decision to quit politics and retire into seclusion came with apparent abruptness. Writing *On Himself*, he gives us a first-hand account of the matter which must be accepted as authoritative, despite the conflicting versions put forward by many of his detractors. Indeed it was in clarification to such versions that he made his statement. He says:

'Here are the facts of that departure. I was in the *Karmayogin* office when I received the word, on information given by a high-placed police official, that the office would be searched the next day and myself arrested. (The office was in fact searched but no warrant was produced against me; I heard nothing more of it till the case was started against the paper later on, but by then I had already left Chandernagore for Pondicherry.) While I was listening to animated comments from those around on the approaching event, I suddenly received a command from above, in a Voice well-known to me, in three words, "Go to Chandernagore". In ten minutes or so I was in the boat for Chandernagore.

. . . Afterwards, under the same "sailing orders" I left Chandernagore and reached Pondicherry on April 4, 1910."[1]

He adds this very interesting and revealing comment:

'From the time I left Lele at Bombay after the Surat Sessions and my stay with him in Baroda, Poona and Bombay, I had accepted the rule of following the inner guidance implicitly and moving only as I was moved by the Divine. The spiritual development during the year in jail had turned this into an absolute law of the being. This accounts for my immediate action in obedience to the Adesh received by me.'[2]

This explains the whole matter in a nutshell, and is fully in consonance with his psychological development during this period. The issue was confused by the fact that after over *eight months* since it was first published, the Government had launched a third prosecution against Sri Aurobindo for his 'Open Letter' and this prosecution almost synchronized with his departure for Chandernagore. The Government of course alleged that Sri Aurobindo had made a precipitate flight in order to avoid arrest. Sri Aurobindo, on his part, issued a statement through the columns of the *Madras Times* in which, as one of his biographers puts it, he explained that he 'had not sought to avoid the long arm of the law; he had only retired to Pondicherry in answer to an imperative inner need to pursue the path of Yoga; the warrant for his arrest had been issued *after* he had already reached Pondicherry; he was therefore not obliged to appear before a British Indian court of justice.'[3]

Two points emerge clearly from the material presented in this chapter. The first is that it is quite unjustified to say that Sri Aurobindo's sudden and dramatic withdrawal from active politics was due to his frustration at seeing the nationalist movement shattered during his year in detention, or to his fear of being re-arrested. His speeches and actions after his release from jail, specially the launching of the *Karmayogin* and the content of that journal, made it abundantly clear that he had lost neither faith nor courage. In fact they show a remarkable up-

[1] *Sri Aurobindo on Himself and on the Mother* (Ashrama), pp. 95-96.

[2] *Ibid.* It is significant and interesting to note that Mahatma Gandhi also was at crucial junctures guided by what he called his 'inner voice'.

[3] *Sri Aurobindo* (Iyengar), pp. 190-91.

surge of power welling up from some deep spiritual fount within him.

The second point is that his departure for Chandernagore and then Pondicherry, though apparently abrupt and as he has himself testified in deference to a compelling higher command, can in fact be accepted as a logical progression from his earlier approach to political problems. Right from the Baroda period he showed a marked spiritual inclination which inevitably reflected itself in his political thought. At the time of the Bengal partition, when he moved to Calcutta and jumped into the political cauldron there, this spiritual approach continued to be prominent in his writings. As we have seen while studying his views on the Nation and Nationalism, his whole concept of political action and theory was based on his spiritual vision, which did not desert him even in the midst of the most extreme and turbulent political controversies of the day. Then came the Surat session and his meeting with Lele, which marked a considerable advance in his spiritual practices and experiences. Soon after came his year of enforced seclusion at Alipur, where it seems that the spiritual tendencies and powers latent in his psyche rose with a dramatic upsurge to the surface. It is in the very nature of the spiritual call that it is imperative and overriding, and if it develops inevitably dominates the mind of the seeker to the virtual exclusion of other activities. Thus we find that the spiritual element in Sri Aurobindo's thinking became predominant, and the over-riding importance that he had attached to current political problems gradually receded.

He began to realize that the real solution to the numerous problems that beset India and mankind in general, including political problems, lay elsewhere than in the noisy midst of day-to-day political controversies. In fact it may be said that he had by 1910 transcended politics in the narrow sense of the word. Thus the 'spiritual nationalism' that was the key-note of Sri Aurobindo's political philosophy led him untimately to eschew politics itself and to seek in spiritual development the ultimate reconciliation, not only for himself, not only for Bengal, not only for India, but for all mankind. The last forty years of his life, from 1910 to 1950, were spent in an effort to hasten the realization of this noble and lofty ideal.

K

PART V

ASSESSMENT OF SRI AUROBINDO
AS A POLITICAL THINKER

ASSESSMENT OF SRI AUROBINDO
AS A POLITICAL THINKER

HAVING surveyed the political thinking of Sri Aurobindo during the period beginning with his return from England in 1893 and ending with his departure for Chandernagore in 1910, we may now attempt a broad assessment of his contribution to modern Indian political thought. This can conveniently be done under four headings: —

1. His concept of spiritual nationalism and the divinity of the Motherland, which imparted an esoteric significance to the movement for India's liberation;

2. His exposition of the ideal of complete freedom from foreign rule, and his role in invigorating, inspiring and radicalizing the national movement;

3. His contribution to the theory of boycott and passive resistance, as also to the use of force if necessary to achieve freedom;

4. His vision of the broader role that India was destined to play in world affairs, and his enlightened ideal of human unity that must ultimately transcend mere national development.

These aspects have been studied in some detail in the body of this work. Here it will only be necessary to sum up the notable contributions made by Sri Aurobindo.

1. We may take first his concept of spiritual nationalism and the divinity of the Motherland. This indeed is the bedrock of his political theory, and underlies all his writings in this field. The divinity of the Motherland is, of course, a concept that has existed since the dawn of history. In the earliest religious texts, not only of India but of other ancient civilizations, the earth— particularly that portion of it occupied by the tribe or society in question—was worshipped as the sustainer, nourisher and

148

supporter of all life and prosperity. The Vedas contain numerous hymns in adoration of the earth, and the worship of *prithvi* is one of the essential rituals in Hindu religious ceremonies. This tradition continued unbroken in India right down to modern times, when Bankim Chandra Chatterjee in his *Ānanda Math* created the famous *mantra* 'Bande Mātaram' glorifying the divinity of the Motherland. Sri Aurobindo's contribution was to take up this mystic and religious concept, adapt it to the political requirements of India at the turn of the century, and turn it into a veritable dynamo of strength and inspiration. His exposition of the religion of nationalism and the consequent necessity for utter self-sacrifice and immolation at the feet of Mother India was unsurpassed for its deeply-felt eloquence. Brief though his political career was, he defined the essence of spiritual nationalism in a manner which for sheer power and passion has perhaps never been equalled. He thus imparted a new dimension to the national movement, lifting it above the purely material plane and placing before it an inspired and inspiring spiritual ideal. It was his *Bhawāni Mandir* that became the gospel of Indian revolutionaries, and it was with a smile and the cry of *Bande Mātaram* on their lips that thousands of patriots faced repression and even death at the hands of their foreign rulers. His concept of the whole National movement is beautifully summed up in his own words: 'The strength of the new movement in India lies in its supreme idealism. It is not a mere economic movement, though it openly strives for the economic resurrection of the country. It is not a mere political movement, though it has boldly declared itself for absolute political independence. It is an intensely spiritual movement having for its object not simply the development of economic life or the attainment of political freedom, but really the emancipation in every sense of the term of the Indian manhood and womanhood.'[1] Sri Aurobindo's contribution to the creation of this 'supreme idealism' was very considerable.

2. Next, we may turn to his second achievement as a political thinker, that is his exposition of the ideal of complete freedom from foreign rule and his role in radicalizing the national move-

[1] 'The Bed-rock of Indian Nationalism'—*Bande Mātaram*, weekly edition, June 14, 1908.

ment. Despite the brevity of his political career, Sri Aurobindo did enough to infuse a new spirit into the movement and thus to help change the very complexion of politics in the country. We have seen how as early as 1893-94, in 'New Lamps for Old', he laid out a radical philosophy of politics. Later his tireless dedicated activity helped to politically galvanize the people of Bengal during the anti-partition agitation. The key to his great influence upon men and events is to be found in the fact that he laid before the people a worthwhile ideal, the ideal of *Purna Swarāj*, complete independence. He had the courage to demand this freedom openly, not as a favour from her alien rulers but as the inalienable birthright of India. His concept of the divinity of the Motherland led directly and inevitably to the demand for her complete emancipation from foreign rule, and Sri Aurobindo preached this doctrine with immense patriotic fervour. Not only did he powerfully advocate the ideal of independence, he also effectively demolished the timid and constricted political platform of the Moderates. Pouring scorn and biting sarcasm upon the 'mendicant' policies of the Moderates, his writings went a long way towards isolating them from the support of public opinion and making the Indian mind receptive to a more radical political programme.

It must also be mentioned that Sri Aurobindo was one of the first Indian leaders to recognize the absolute necessity of generating mass enthusiasm and participation in the national cause, of getting the support of all the varied constituents of the Indian body politic, in other words, of democratizing the whole movement. As early as 1893 he clearly enunciated this view, and trenchantly criticized the Congress for remaining a confined and narrow organization without any mass support. He is thus one of the earliest true democrats on the modern Indian scene.

Another facet of his thought which enabled him to impart fresh spirit into the national movement was his stress on the necessity for suffering by the children before their Mother could be liberated. Unlike the proper, prim and correct conservatives who thought that the British would out of their own charity and beneficence grant India the loaf of freedom crumb by crumb, Sri Aurobindo knew and stressed clearly the necessity for a 'purification by blood and fire' before the goal could be attained. His stress on the goal of complete independence, his theory of the divinity of the Motherland and the almost religious character of the liberation movement, his emphasis upon the necessity of suffering and sacrifice to achieve the goal, all combined to impart a revolutionary spirit to the whole struggle against British domination. His flaming advocacy of India's right to be free swept aside the more modest goals of the moderates and cut them off from the main stream of public support.

Yet another factor in his thought which helped to revitalize the spirit of India was his profound reappraisal of the true springs of Indian culture, of the true greatness of her spiritual heritage. His writings, combining as they did startling erudition with flaming patriotic fervour, caused a stir among the intelligentsia. Of all the great leaders of the Radical movement, Sri Aurobindo's literary talent was by far the most impressive, and this enabled him effectively to transmit his dream of the future India to receptive and anxious minds. At the same time his forceful writing helped to break the myth of British cultural superiority so assiduously fostered by the foreign rulers. His contribution towards creating a climate of revolutionary nationalism in India directed at securing her complete independence from foreign rule was very substantial. He was indeed, as Tagore so eloquently put it, the 'Voice incarnate free, of India's soul'.

A word may here be said about a criticism levelled against Sri Aurobindo and other Radical leaders that they neglected the important issue of social reform. It is true that they did not lay very much emphasis upon this aspect of public life which has now assumed so much significance, but this was not because they considered social reform unimportant. It was rather because they were convinced of the primary necessity of securing political independence before a really effective scheme of social reform could be attempted with any hope of success. They recognized the importance of such reform, but felt that it could not precede political independence. To attempt social reform before becoming independent would not only be to put the cart before the horse, but also to fritter away energies that could more usefully be yoked to the national movement itself. It was this view, and not any aversion to social reform *per se*, that led Sri Aurobindo to attack the Moderate leadership for their obsession with social problems.

3. In this assessment of Sri Aurobindo as a political thinker we

may turn now to his contribution to the theory of boycott and passive resistance. This has been treated at some length in this work, and we have seen how he was not only a theorist but a masterly political tactician. His voluminous writings on boycott contain a comprehensive exposition of the theory in its many facets. At the same time he made concrete suggestions about the positive steps that must accompany boycott if it was to be really effective. Thus along with his theory of economic boycott he postulated the necessity of *swadeshi*; along with educational boycott he put forward his views of national education; along with judicial boycott he stressed the necessity for national arbitration courts; along with executive boycott he expounded the importance of national organization; and as the sanction behind the whole boycott theory he placed the concept of social boycott. Sri Aurobindo was one of those rare thinkers whose thought was not confined only to the theoretical implications of a problem but who descended into the arena of life and tested his theories against the actual demands of practical politics.

A word may here be said about his advocacy of force and violence if necessary in the struggle against foreign domination. This is sometimes levelled against him as a criticism, and it is said he was an anarchist and a terrorist. As for his being an anarchist, the proposition can be dismissed out of hand as absurd. He sought to replace British rule not by anarchy but by national rule. Regarding his terrorism, there is now little doubt that he was not only closely in touch with secret revolutionary groups throughout the country but, in Bengal, was for a considerable time their secret leader and inspirer. This charge, if such it can be termed, is one which is fully in consonance with his basic political theory. Which son, if his mother was being crushed and humiliated by an alien aggressor, would hesitate to use every means including force and violence to effect her deliverance? For Sri Aurobindo the deliverance of the Motherland from foreign rule was the one paramount, over-riding consideration. To this end all means were admissible, including violence, specially when the foreigners themselves were in India as the result of forcible conquest.

4. Finally, we come to his lofty ideal of human unity and of India's destined role in the international community. Although his exposition and elaboration of this concept took place mainly after 1910, and thus lies beyond the scope of this work, we have

seen that even in the 1893-1910 period it is clearly brought out in his political writings. Thus, when discussing the theoretical compulsions behind Sri Aurobindo's political goal of complete independence, we saw that an important factor in his thought was the conviction that India must be free not for herself alone, but for the benefit of entire mankind. He felt that India had a spiritual message which was urgently needed in the world of the twentieth century, in fact that she was destined to lead mankind up the next step of spiritual evolution, and one of the reasons why he was so adamant that the political goal should be nothing less than complete independence was his conviction that then alone could India fulfil her true destiny in the broader international community.

At a time when India was firmly and securely under British rule, and the prospect of her becoming free appeared extremely dim, it is a tribute to Sri Aurobindo's breadth of vision that he was able clearly to foresee her destiny as a free nation, and to stress the importance of the contribution that she must make to the world community. Thus, in his celebrated 'Open Letter to My Countrymen' written in 1909, he says:

'Our ideal of patriotism proceeds on the basis of love and brotherhood and it looks beyond the unity of the nation and envisages the ultimate unity of mankind. But it is a unity of brothers, equals and free men that we seek, not the unity of master and serf, of devourer and devoured.'[1]

This lofty idealism in a way pre-mirrored the importance that free India has given to the maintenance of world peace, and the special role she has played therein. Sri Aurobindo's nationalism never descended into narrow chauvinism or obscurantist re-vivalism. It was constantly placed in a broader international context, and even in the white heat of political controversy he never lost sight of his ideal of human unity which far transcended local problems and had for its goal the ultimate reconciliation of all conflicts in a syncretic spiritual development. This theme in fact recurs in almost all his writings, from the

[1] *Speeches*, p. 142. In his political writings Sri Aurobindo lays great stress upon this broader aspect of Indian nationalism. See, for example, Editorials in the *Bande Mātaram* on 'The Asiatic Role' (April 12, 1908), 'The New Ideal' (April 12, 1908), 'Ideals Face to Face' (May 3, 1908), 'The Bedrock of Indian Nationalism' (June 4, 1908).

early passion of *Bhavāni Mandir* and *Bande Mātaram* to the mature reflections of his later monumental works such as *The Ideal of Human Unity, Essays on the Gita* and *The Life Divine,* and must be classed as one of his major contributions to modern Indian political theory. Although at the time he wrote the idea had mainly academic interest, as India was not in fact free, yet it had the effect of raising the whole tone of the national movement and placing before it an ideal even more elevated than that of national independence. That his ideal of human unity has to some extent been realized is a tribute to Sri Aurobindo's wisdom; that it has still not been fully translated into action is the measure of mankind's failure to rise to its full stature.

Sri Aurobindo thus emerges as a political thinker of great importance in modern Indian political thought. He was largely responsible for imparting an esoteric and spiritual significance to the national movement, for placing before it the inspiring ideal of complete independence, for invigorating the spirit of India by a reassessment of the true bases of her great cultural heritage, for expounding a practical system whereby the goal of independence could be achieved, and for placing the whole movement in the broader context of internationalism and the ideal of humany unity. For a person to have done this in the short period of hardly five years of active political life is an achievement of no mean importance. Sri Aurobindo must be counted among the great builders of modern India, as he contributed nobly towards laying the foundations for the edifice of national freedom which Mahatma Gandhi and others later reared. Even after 1910 his interest in Indian freedom remained undiminished, and he lived to see the fruition of his work when India finally achieved Independence on his seventy-fifty birthday, the fifteenth of August, 1947.

APPENDIX

THE FIFTEENTH OF AUGUST, 1947

AUGUST 15th, 1947, is the birthday of free India. It marks for her the end of an old era, the beginning of a new age. But we can also make it by our life and acts as a free nation an important date in a new age opening for the whole world, for the political, social, cultural and spiritual future of humanity.

August 15th is my own birthday and it is naturally gratifying to me that it should have assumed this vast significance. I take this coincidence, not as a fortuitous accident, but as the sanction and seal of the Divine Force that guides my steps on the work with which I began life, the beginning of its full fruition. Indeed, on this day I can watch almost all the world-movements which I hoped to see fulfilled in my lifetime, though then they looked like impracticable dreams, arriving at fruition or on their way to achievement. In all these movements free India may well play a large part and take a leading position.

The first of these dreams was a revolutionary movement which would create a free and united India. India today is free but she has not achieved unity. At one moment it almost seemed as if in the very act of liberation she would fall back into the chaos of separate States which preceded the British conquest. But fortunately it now seems probable that this danger will be averted and a large and powerful, though not yet a complete union will be established. Also, the wisely drastic policy of the Constituent Assembly has made it probable that the problem of the depressed classes will be solved without schism or fissure. But the old communal division into Hindus and Muslims seems now to have hardened into a permanent political division of the country. It is to be hoped that this settled fact will not be accepted as settled for ever or as anything more than a temporary expedient. For if it lasts, India may be seriously weakened, even crippled: civil strife may remain always possible, possible even a new invasion and foreign conquest. India's internal development and prosperity may be impeded, her position among the nations weakened, her destiny impaired or even frustrated. This must not be; the partition must go. Let us hope that that may come about naturally, by an increasing recognition of the necessity not only of peace and concord but of common action, by the practice of common action and the creation of means for that purpose. In this way unity may finally come about under whatever form—the exact form may have a pragmatic but not a fundamental importance. But by whatever means, in whatever way, the division must go; unity must and will be achieved, for it is necessary for the greatness of India's future.

Another dream was for the resurgence and liberation of the peoples of Asia and her return to her great role in the progress of human civilization. Asia has arisen; large parts are now quite free or are at this moment being liberated: its other still subject or partly subject parts are moving through whatever struggles towards freedom. Only a little has to be done and that will be done today or tomorrow. There India has her part to play and has begun to play it with an energy and ability which already indicate the measure of her possibilities and the place she can take in the council of the nations.

The third dream was a world-union forming the outer basis of a fairer, brighter and nobler life for all mankind. That unification of the human world is under way; there is an imperfect initiation organized but struggling against tremendous difficulties. But the momentum is there and it must inevitably increase and conquer. Here too India has begun to play a prominent part and, if she can develop that larger statesmanship which is not limited by the present facts and immediate possibilities but looks into the future and brings it nearer, her presence may make all the difference between a slow and timid and a bold and swift development. A catastrophe may intervene and interrupt or destroy what is being done, but even then the final result is sure. For unification is a necessity of Nature, an inevitable movement. Its necessity for the nations is also clear, for without it the freedom of the small nations may be at any moment in peril and the life even of the large and powerful nations insecure. The unification is therefore to the interests of all, and only human imbecility and stupid selfishness can prevent it; but these cannot stand for ever against the necessity of Nature and the Divine Will. But an outward basis is not enough; there must grow up an international spirit and outlook, international forms and institutions must appear, perhaps such developments as dual or multilateral citizenship, willed interchange or voluntary fusion of cultures. Nationalism will have fulfilled itself and lost its militancy and would no longer find these things incompatible with self-preservation and the integrality of its outlook. A new spirit of oneness will take hold of the human race.

Another dream, the spiritual gift of India to the world has already begun. India's spirituality is entering Europe and America in an ever-increasing measure. That movement will grow; amid the disasters of the time more and more eyes are turning towards her with hope and there is even an increasing resort not only to her teachings, but to her psychic and spiritual practice.

The final dream was a step in evolution which would raise man to a higher and larger consciousness and begin the solution of the problems which have perplexed and vexed him since he first began to think and to dream of individual perfection and a perfect society. This is still a personal hope and an idea, an ideal which has begun to take hold both in India and in the West on forward-looking minds. The difficulties in the way are more formidable than in any other field of endeavour, but difficulties were made to be overcome and if the Supreme Will is there, they will be overcome. Here too, if this evolution is to take place, since it must proceed through a growth of the spirit and the inner consciousness the initiative can come from India and, although the scope must be universal, the central movement may be hers.

Such is the content which I put into this date of India's liberation; whether or how far this hope will be justified depends upon the new and free India.

BIBLIOGRAPHY

A

WORKS BY SRI AUROBINDO GHOSH
(Unless otherwise indicated, these works have been published by the Sri Aurobindo Ashrama, Pondicherry.)

1. *Bankim Chandra Chatterjee* (1954)
2. *Bankim-Tilak-Dayananda* (1955)
3. *'Bhawāni Mandir'*
   (published in Sri Aurobindo Mandir *Annual* Jayanti Number No. 15, August 15, 1956, Sri Aurobindo Pathamandir, Calcutta)
4. *The Brain of India* (5th Edition 1955)
5. *Collected Poems and Plays* (2 volumes) (1942)
6. *The Doctrine of Passive Resistance* (2nd Ed. 1952)
7. *Eight Upanishadas* (1953)
8. *Elements of Yoga* (1953)
9. *Essays on the Gita*
   (Sri Aurobindo Library, New York) (1950)
10. *Evolution* (5th Edition 1950)
11. *The Foundations of Indian Culture*
    (Sri Aurobindo Library, New York) (1953)
12. *The Human Cycle*
    (Sri Aurobindo Library, New York (1950)
13. *The Ideal of Human Unity*
    (Sri Aurobindo Library, New York (1950)
14. *The Ideal of Karmayogi* (7th Edition 1950)
15. *Ideals and Progress* (4th Edition 1951)
16. *Letters* (4th Series): 1st Series 2nd Edition 1950; 2nd Series 1949; 3rd Series 1949; 4th Series 1951

17. *The Life Divine*
    (Sri Aurobindo Library, New York) (2nd Printing 1951)
18. *Conversations of the Dead* (1951)
19. *On Himself and on the Mother* (1953)
20. *The Renaissance in India* (4th Edition 1951)
21. *The Riddle of this World* (4th Edition 1951)
22. *The Significance of Indian Art* (2nd Edition 1953)
23. *Speeches* (3rd Edition 1952)
24. *The Spirit and Form of Indian Polity* (1947)
25. *The Superman* (4th Edition 1950)
26. *Thoughts and Glimpses* (5th Reprint 1950)
27. *After the War* (1949)
28. Articles by Sri Aurobindo in *Bande Mātaram* Weekly (1907-1908) and *Karmayogin* (1909-1910). Many of these articles are now completely out of print and un- available to the general public. Through my friend Syed Mehdi Imam I was able to secure over two hundred such articles from the Archives of the Sri Aurobindo Ashrama at Pondicherry. These articles, written as they were in the very midst of the political controversy in Bengal, are of immense value in a study of the political thought of Sri Aurobindo during that period. I have made considerable use of this rare material in the preparation of this thesis, and have quoted often from these articles.

B

OTHER WORKS

1. BARNES, MARGARITA, *The Indian Press*, George Allen & Unwin Ltd., London (1940)
2. BHARATI, SHUDDHANANDA, *Sri Aurobindo, the Divine Master*, Pudu Yuga Nilayam, Pondicherry (2nd Revised edition 1948)
3. BHATTACHARYYA, HARIDAS (Editor), *The Cultural Heritage of India* (Volume IV), The Ramakrishna Mission Institute of Culture (1956)
4. BROWN, D. MACKENZIE, *The White Umbrella*, University of California (1953)

5. BUCH, M. A., *The Development of Contemporary Indian Political Thought* (Volume III), Good Companions, Baroda (1940)

6. CHATTERJEE, BANKIM CHANDRA, *Ānanda Math* (Translated by Sri Aurobindo Ghosh and Barindra Kumar Ghosh), Basumati Sahitya Mandir, Calcutta

7. CHINTAMANI, C. Y., *Indian Politics since the Mutiny*, Kitabistan, Allahabad (1947)

8. CHIROL, VALENTINE, *Indian Unrest*, Macmillan, London (1910)

9. DE BARY, WM. THEODORE (Editor), *Sources of Indian Tradition*, Columbia University Press (1958)

10. DE REINCOURT, AMAURY, *The Soul of India*, Harper & Brothers, New York (1960)

11. DESAI, A. R., *Social Background of Indian Nationalism*, Popular Book Depot, Bombay (3rd Edition 1959)
Recent Trends in Indian Nationalism, Popular Book Depot, Bombay (1960)

12. DIWAKAR, R. R., Mahayogi, Bharatiya Vidya Bhavan, Bombay (1954)

13. DONNELLY, MORWENNA, *Founding the Life Divine*, Rider & Company, London (1955)

14. DUTT, C. C., *The Culture of India as envisaged by Sri Aurobindo*, Bharatiya Vidya Bhavan, Bombay (1960)

15. DUTT, R. PALME, *India Today*, People's Publishing House, Bombay (2nd Revised Indian Edition 1949)

16. GHOSE, HEMENDRA PRASAD, *Aurobindo—The Prophet of Patriotism*, A. K. Mitter, Calcutta (1949)

17. GHOSH, P. C., *Indian National Congress*, Firma K. L. Mukhopadhyaya, Calcutta (1960)

18. GOKHALE, B. G., *The Making of the Indian Nation*, Asia Publishing House (2nd Edition 1960)

19. GRIFFITHS, SIR PERCIVAL, *The British Impact on India*, Macdonald, London (1952)

20. GUPTA, NOLINI KANTA, *The Yoga of Sri Aurobindo* (9 parts), Sri Aurobindo Ashrama, Pondicherry (1958)
Sri Aurobindo and his Ashrama, Sri Aurobindo Ashrama, Pondicherry (1951)
The Message of Sri Aurobindo and the Ashrama, Sri Aurobindo Niketan, New Delhi (1951)

21. IYENGAR, K. R. SRINIVASA, *Sri Aurobindo*, Arya Publishing House, Calcutta (1950)
Sri Aurobindo, An Introduction, Rao and Raghavan, Mysore (1961)

22. KARMARKAR, D. P., *Bal Gangadhar Tilak*, Popular Book Depot, Bombay (1956)

23. LOVETT, SIR VERNEY, *A History of the Indian National Movement*, John Murray, London (1920)

24. MAITRA, S. K., *The Meeting of the East and the West in Sri Aurobindo's Philosophy*, Sri Aurobindo Ashrama, Pondicherry (1956)

25. MAJUMDAR, R. C., *Three Phases of India's Struggle for Freedom*, Bharatiya Vidya Bhavan, Bombay (1961)

26. MARY, COUNTESS OF MINTO, *India: Minto and Morley* (1905-1910), Macmillan, London (1934)

27. MITRA, SISIR KUMAR, *Sri Aurobindo and Indian Freedom*, Sri Aurobindo Library, Madras (1948)
Sri Aurobindo and the New World, Sri Aurobindo Ashrama, Pondicherry (1957)
The Liberator, Jaico, Bombay (1954)
The Dawn Eternal, Sri Aurobindo Ashrama, Pondicherry (1954)

28. MUKHERJEES, PROFESSORS HARIDAS & UMA, *The Origins of the National Education Movement* (1905-1910), Jadavpur University, Calcutta (1957)
Bande Mataram and Indian Nationalism (1906-1908), Firma K. L. Mukhopadhyaya, Calcutta (1957)
Sri Aurobindo's Political Thought (1893-1908), Firma K. L. Mukhopadhyaya, Calcutta (1958)
India's Fight for Freedom or *The Swadeshi Movement* (1905-1906), Firma K. L. Mukhopadhyaya, Calcutta (1958)
A Phase of the Swadeshi Movement (National Education 1905-1910), Chukerverty, Chatterjee & Co. Ltd., Calcutta
Bipin Chandra Pal, Firma K. L. Mukhopadhyaya (1958)

29. PANIKKAR, K. M., *A Survey of Indian History*, Asia Publishing House, Bombay (Second Edition 1944)
Commonsense about India, Macmillan, New York (1960)

30. PEARSON, NATHANIEL, *Sri Aurobindo and the Soul Quest of Man*, George Allen & Unwin Ltd., London (1952)

31. PRADHAN, G. P. and BHAGWAT, A. K., *Lokamanya Tilak*, Jaico, Bombay (1959)

32. PURANI, A. B., *Life of Sri Aurobindo*, Sri Aurobindo Ashrama, Pondicherry (1958)
Sri Aurobindo in England, Sri Aurobindo Ashrama, Pondicherry (1956)

33. RAMGOPAL, *Lokamanya Tilak*, Asia Publishing House, Bombay (1956)

34. REYMOND, LIZELLE, *The Dedicated, a biography of Nivedita*, The John Day Company, New York (1953)

35. ROY, DILIP KUMAR, *Among the Great*, Jaico, Bombay (1950)

36. SHARMA, BISHAN SARUP, *Gandhi as a Political Thinker*, Indian Press (Publications) Private Ltd., Allahabad (1956)

37. SHAY, THEODORE L., *The Legacy of the Lokamanya*, Oxford University Press (1956)

38. SITARAMAYYA, B. PATTABHI, *History of the Indian National Congress*, Volume I (1885-1935), Padma Publications Ltd., Bombay (1946)

39. TAGORE, RABINDRANATH, *Salutation to Sri Aurobindo*, Sri Aurobindo Ashrama, Pondicherry (1959)

40. TAHMANKAR, D. V., *Lokamanya Tilak*, John Murray, London (1956)

41. VARMA, V. P., *The Political Philosophy of Sri Aurobindo*, Asia Publishing House, Bombay (1960)

42. VIJAYATUNGA, J., *Aspects of Sri Aurobindo*, Sunday Times Bookshop, Madras

C

REPORTS AND FILES

1. Indian National Congress:
   a Report of the 17th session, Calcutta 1901
   b Report of the 18th session, Allahabad 1902
   c Report of the 19th session, Madras 1903
   d Report of the 20th session, Bombay 1904
   e Report of the 21st session, Banaras 1905
   f Report of the 22nd session, Calcutta 1906
   g Report of the 23rd session, Madras 1908 (including proceedings of the session held at Surat in 1907)

2. Government of India Home Department file Nos. 230-248, October, 1909, and file No. 566-1909. These files were secured from the National Archives of India, and deal with the proposed appeal by the Government of India against Sri Aurobindo's acquittal in the Alipore Bomb Conspiracy Case.

D

ARTICLES

1. CHAKRAVARTI, P. C., 'Sri Aurobindo and the Indian Freedom Movement' in *Loving Homage*, Sri Aurobindo Pathamandir, Calcutta (1958)
   'Genesis of the Partition of Bengal (1905)', in *The Modern Review*, April, 1959
2. DAS, TARAK NATH, 'The Political Philosophy of Sri Aurobindo', in *The Integral Philosophy of Sri Aurobindo*, George Allen & Unwin Ltd., London (1960)
3. KARAN SINGH, 'Sri Aurobindo and the Indian Renaisance' in *Varied Rhythms*, Asia Publishing House, Bombay (1960)
4. MUKHERJEES, PROFESSORS HARIDAS and UMA, 'The Ideologies of the Swadeshi Movement', *Hindustan Standard Sunday Magazine*, October 11, 1953.
5. MUNSHI, K. M., 'Sri Aurobindo—An Appreciation', The *Hindustan Times*, New Delhi, December 6, 1950.
6. ROY, ANILBARAN, 'Sri Aurobindo and Religious Education', *Amrit Bazar Patrika*, Calcutta, December 5, 1951.
7. Tributes to Sri Aurobindo: *Amrit Bazar Patrika*, Calcutta, December 6, 1950; *The Hindu*, Madras, December 6, 1950; *Hindustan Standard*, Calcutta, December 6, 1950; *Hindustan Standard*, Calcutta, December 10, 1950; *Hindustan Times*, New Delhi, December 6, 1950

GEORGE ALLEN & UNWIN LTD

London: 40 Museum Street, W.C. 1
Auckland: 24 Wyndham Street
Bombay: 15 Graham Road, Ballard Estate, Bombay 1
Buenos Aires. Escritorio 454-459, Florida 165
Calcutta: 17 Chittaranjan Avenue, Calcutta 13
Cape Town: 109 Long Street
Hong Kong: F1/12 Mirador Mansions, Kowloon
Ibadan: P.O. Box 62
Karachi: Karachi Chambers, McLeod Road
Madras: Mohan Mansions, 38c Mount Road, Madras 6
Mexico: Villalongin 32-10, Piso, Mexico 5, D.F.
Nairobi: P.O. Box 12446
New Delhi: 13-14 Asaf Ali Road, New Delhi 1
Sao Paulo: Avenida 9 de Julho 1138-Ap. 51
Singapore: 36c Prinsep Street, Singapore 7
Sydney: N.S.W.: Bradbury House, 55 York Street
Tokyo: 3 Kanda Ogawamachi 3-chome
Toronto: 91 Wellington Street West